IS PREP

LANGUAGE USAGE (GRAMMAR)

국내 유일 **MAP TEST 학습서**

국제 학교 입시 컨설팅 전문가가 직접 저술한 MAP TEST 가이드

국제 학교 지원생이라면 반드시 공부해야 할 학습서

AROUNZ.ACADEMY

머릿말

MAP Test란?

MAP 테스트는 학생들의 학업 수준을 평가하는 데 사용되는 NWEA에서 개발한 실력 평가 시험입니다. 이 테스트는 유치원부터 12학년까지의 학생들을 대상으로 하며, 국제학교의 입학 시험이나 학교에 입학 후 학생의 학력을 측정하는 데 활용됩니다. 학년별 표준 점수를 비교하여 학생의 학습 진척을 추적하거나, 개별 학생의 강약점을 파악하는 데 도움이 됩니다. 테스트는 대략 2시간소요되며, 컴퓨터 적응형 형식을 채택하여 학생의 답안에 따라 문제의 난이도를 조절합니다.

MAP Test 시험 구성

MAP 테스트는 Language Usage, Reading, Math로 구성되며 객관식, 빈칸 채우기 객관식, 다중 선택, 드래그 앤 드롭 및 기타 유형의 문제등과 같은 다양한 형식의 문제유형이 있습니다. 각 유형별로 40-50문제가 나오며 테스트의 난이도는 학생의 학년 수준으로 시작됩니다. 맞힐 경우 다음 문제는 더 어려워지고 틀릴 경우 다음 문제는 쉬워집니다.

시험이 어렵다고 느꼈을 경우 시험을 잘 본 것으로 여겨집니다. 쉽다고 느끼면 상당히 낮은 레벨까지 내려 간 것이라고 생각하면 됩니다.

RIT 점수 이해하기

시험이 끝난 후 RIT 성적표를 받게 되는데 이것은 학생이 대략 50%의 문제를 정확하게 대답한 수준을 반영합니다

점수 범위: 100~300

제주 국제학교 합격 점수: 245~250

(비인가 학교의 경우 맵 점수로 AP를 들을 수 있을지 정하기도 합니다.

역시 240점 정도 필요합니다.)

MAP Test의 구성

시험영역	출제 지문 및 문항수	점수 범위	특징
Reading	40-43	100-300	문맥속에서 단어의 뜻 유추하기 메인 아이디어 찾기 결론 유추하기 문학작품/ 정보전달 지문: 작가의 의도 파악, 메인 아이디어 찾기, 결론 유추하기, 비유적 언어 이해, Literature device 이해, 요약
Language Usage	50-53	100-300	Writing 영역: 글쓰기를 단계별로 구성 할 수 있는지 다 쓴 후 수정할 수 있는지를 평가 Language: 문법의 사용, 스펠링 철자, 문장 부호, 대문자 사용등의 능력 평가
Math	43-53	100-300	연산 능력, 자리수, 정수, 분수, 비교, 반올림, 데이터 분석 및 해석 (길이, 무게, 액체 체적, 시간, 돈, 면적, 둘레 및 각을 포함하는 측정 문제를 이해하고 해결할 수 있는 능력), 기하학, 그래프

MAP Test 전략

1. 맵테스트에 나오는 단어를 익힌다.

   단기간에 준비를 하는 것이기 때문에 많은 단어를 짧은 시간 동안 외우는 것에는 한계가 있습니다. 맵테스트에 나오는 단어 위주로 외우는 것이 중요합니다. 문법 용어, Literature device 를 파악하고 문제에서 물어보는 것이 무엇인지 아는 것이 중요합니다. 수학용어 또한 익숙해 지는 것이 필요합니다.

2. 메인 아이디어를 찾는 능력을 기른다.

   짧은 시간동안 전체적인 내용을 파악하는 것은 중요합니다. 그러면서 메인 아이디어를 빠르게 찾는 것은 중요합니다. 메인 아이디어가 주로 나오는 위치를 파악하는 것이 중요합니다.

3. 다양한 종류의 리딩을 접해 본다.

   맵테스트의 리딩유형은 다음과 같습니다.

1. Persuative Writing
2. Narrative Writing
3. Expository
4. Descriptive
5. Compare and contrast
6. Reflective
7. Personal
8. Poetry Writing
9. imperative writing

   리딩 유형을 파악하는 것이 중요합니다. 많이 읽고 분석해보아야 합니다.

4. 문제를 많이 풀어본다.

   문제은행에서 출제되기 때문에 다양한 문제를 풀어 봄으로써 문제에 익숙해 질 수 있습니다. 문제 유형을 익혀야 합니다.

5. 오답 노트를 만든다.

   학생의 약한부분을 빠르게 파악하는 것이 중요합니다. 오답 노트를 통해 나의 약점을 빠르게 파악하고 똑같은 문제는 다시 틀리지 않습니다.

   오답노트 만드는 요령

   문제쓰기 (문제에서 중요한 부분을 쓰고 굳이 영어일 필요는 없습니다.)

   답쓰기 그러면서 오답 고치기 (왜 이것이 답인지 이유를 적는 것이 중요합니다.)

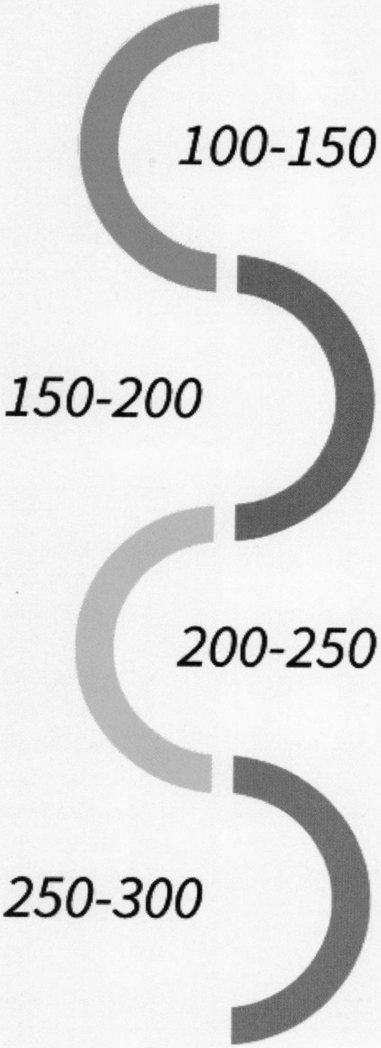

100~150 (처음 시작하는 단계)

문제를 이해하는데 집중합니다.

단어 및 문법 용어에 집중합니다.

150~200

단어를 계속적으로 외웁니다. 오답노트를 통해 잘 틀리는 부분을 파악합니다.

리딩을 많이 읽어봅니다. 그냥 읽는 것이 아니라 메인 아이디어, 요약 쓰는 것을 통한 능동적 리딩을 합니다.

200~250

단어를 계속적으로 외웁니다.

틀린 문제를 안 틀리도록 노력합니다.

리딩 문제를 주어진 시간 보다 더 빠르게 풀고 읽는 연습을 합니다.

250~300

잘 틀리는 단어를 확인합니다.

모의고사를 많이 풀어봅니다.

(3가지 영역을 따로 풀지 말고 함께 계속적으로 실전 시험 보듯이 풀어봅니다.)

CONTENTS

Grammar List

Sentences

a.) Sentences & Fragments
b.) Telling and Commanding sentences
c.) Questions and Exclamatory sentences
d.) Simple and Compound Sentences
e.) Run-on Sentences

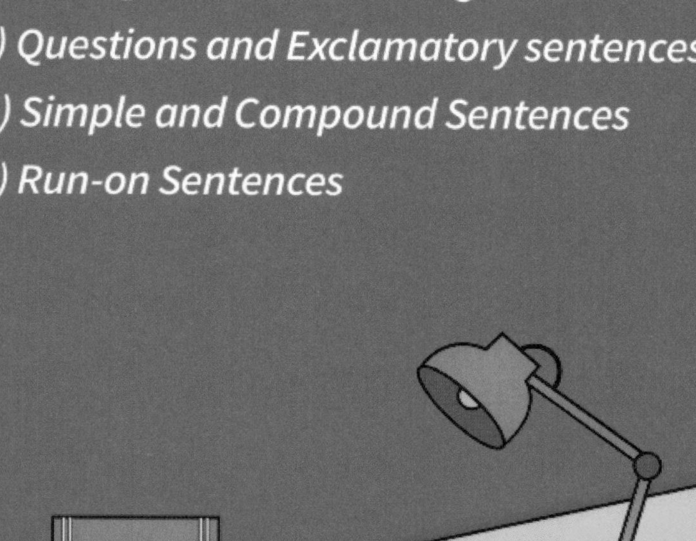

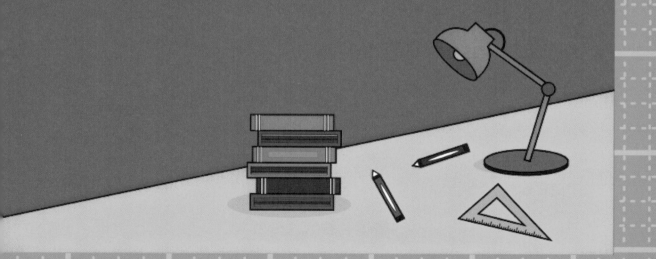

A sentence is a group of words that tells a complete thought. A complete sentence will tell you WHO DOES WHAT/WHERE.

WHO	DOES	WHAT
The man	ate	The cookie

WHO	DOES	WHERE
Horses	run	in the field

Sentence and Fragment Practice: Put the words in order to make a complete sentence. Remember, a sentence tells **WHO DOES WHAT/WHERE** and starts with a capital letter.

1. to music | The girl | listens | .

____

2. Jenni | in a bunk bed | sleeps | .

____

3. My mother | in the park | . | enjoys walking

____

4. . | are playing | The children | in the park

____

5. in the kitchen | . | is | The dog

____

If a sentence is missing one of its three parts, it is not a complete sentence. Instead this is a **fragment**.

This sentence has all of the necessary parts and is complete.

WHO	DOES	WHERE
The boy	is looking	out of the window

This is a fragment because only two parts of the sentence are here.

WHO	DOES	WHERE
The boy	is looking	

WHO	DOES	WHERE
	Looking	out of the window

Practice: Read the fragments below. Circle the part of the sentence they are missing and then fix it on the line.

The lion ate	who	does	what/where
caught fist	who	does	what/where
My teacher	who	does	what/where

Practice: Read the phrase. If it is a complete sentence circle S if it is a fragment circle F.

1. He is my idol.	S	F
2. I need a pen.	S	F
3. The baton twirlers.	S	F
4. The food is here.	S	F
5. In the parade.	S	F
6. Before the parade passes by.	S	F
7. I don't know what to do.	S	F
8. This is the way!	S	F
9. Fire away!	S	F
10. We are great friends.	S	F

Practice: Write five complete sentences. Remember a complete sentence tells WHO DOES WHAT/WHERE.

1. ____________________

2. ____________________

3. ____________________

4. ____________________

5. ____________________

Sentences: Subjects and Predicates

You know that a complete sentence tells WHO DOES WHAT. The WHO part of a sentence is called the SUBJECT.

Jenine likes juice.
She likes juice.
My friend, Jenine, likes juice.

Practice: Underline the subject in each sentence.

Amanda likes to play soccer.

Ben wants to go to a soccer game.

Amanda and Ben will watch the Tottenham game this weekend!

They are playing against Chelsea.

The game starts at 3 o'clock.

Complete the sentences by adding a subject to the given predicate.

1. ______________________

2. ______________________

3. ______________________

4. ______________________

5. ______________________

The DOES WHAT part of a sentence is called the predicate.

Jenine likes juice.

She drinks juice everyday.

My friend, Jenine, wants to learn to make her own juice.

Practice: Underline the predicate in each sentence.

1. Jay is painting a tree.
2. Rachel is sitting in front of the tree.
3. Michael will meet them in the park later.
4. Jay will add Rachel and Michael to his painting.
5. He wants to be a painter in the future.

Add a predicate to complete the sentence.

6. Vincent Van Gogh ________________________________.
7. He ________________________________.
8. Many people ________________________________.
9. Starry Night ________________________________.
10. Painting ________________________________.

Sentences: Statements and Commands

A **declarative sentence** is a **statement** that tells about something and ends with a period. These follow the format: SUBJECT + ACTION + VERB.

The baby is asleep. **The ball is red.** **We walked to the store.**

An **imperative sentence is a command** that tells someone to do something. Usually, a command ends with a period but if it shows a strong feeling, it can end with an exclamation point. It is also common for a command to not have a subject.

Don't touch that! **Zip your coat.** **Write your name on your paper.**

Practice: Read the sentence. If it is a statement sentence circle S if it is a command, circle C.

Open the door.	S	C
My sister likes Mac and Cheese.	S	C
Eat your vegetables.	S	C
Flowers bloom in spring.	S	C
I haven't read that book.	S	C
Don't write in the book!	S	C
He is a very good dancer.	S	C
Practice your scales.	S	C
Tell me about your family.	S	C
That is a really good book.	S	C

Sentences: Questions

An **interrogative sentence** is a question that asks something and ends with a question mark.

Do you like bananas? **Is he your brother?** **Where is your book?**

There are two main types of questions. The first is the **Wh Question.** These questions start with one of the five "Wh Words".

Wh Words				
Who	What	When	Where	Why
Who is going to the party?	What is the party for?	When is the party?	Where is the party?	Why aren't you going?

Practice: Fill in the blank with the correct Wh Word and answer the question for yourself.

1. _________ is your birthday? _______________________________
2. _________ is your age? _______________________________
3. _________ is your father's name? _______________________________
4. _________ is sitting next to you? _______________________________
5. _________ are you learning English? _______________________________
6. _________ do you live? _______________________________

Another type of question is the **Yes/No Question.** These are questions that require a simple yes or no answer.

Do you like Mint Chocolate ice cream?

Yes, it's my favorite flavor. | No, I think it's disgusting

Format: Helping verb + Subject + verb + object.
Common Helping verbs: do/does or have/has

Practice: Answer the question about you and your family.

1. Have you been to America? ______________________
2. Do you like broccoli? ______________________
3. Do you have a sister? ______________________
4. Do you like Indian food? ______________________
5. Have you tried escargot? ______________________

Practice: Write the question asked based on the answer given.

6. ______________________ Yes, I like cheesecake.
7. ______________________ No, I haven't been to Africa.
8. ______________________ No, I don't have a cat.
9. ______________________ Yes, I like Sci-fi movies.
10. ______________________ No, I don't like poetry.

An **exclamatory sentence** is an **exclamation.** It is similar to a statement, but it shows surprise or excitement and ends with an exclamation point.

We're going to Disneyland! **This pizza is amazing!** **I won the contest!**

Practice: Circle the correct ending mark for the sentence.

1. Are you hungry	?	!
2. I love chocolate	?	!
3. Do you speak Spanish	?	!
4. SURPRISE	?	!
5. Sonny was here	?	!
6. Where is the remote	?	!
7. I'm the king of the world	?	!
8. Where does he live	?	!
9. Would you like to go to the movies	?	!
10. That's my favorite movie	?	!

Sentence Type Review:

Which sentence is a statement?

a.) What color is the car?

b.) Look out for the car!

c.) This is my car.

Which sentence is an interrogative sentence?

a.) Look at the monkeys!

b.) Monkeys are my favorite animal.

c.) Do you like monkeys?

Which sentence is a question?

a.)This is my hat.

b.) Where is my hat?

c.) Don't forget your hat!

Which sentence is a statement?

a.)I went to the movies last night.

b.) What movie did you see?

c.) It was so exciting!

Which sentence is an exclamation?

a.) I love this song!

b.) Do you know this song?

c.) I can play this song on guitar.

Which sentence is a command?

a.) Do your homework!

b.) Did you do your homework?

c.) My homework is hard.

Which sentence is a command?

a.) I'll call you tonight.

b.) Call me tonight.

c.) Will you call me tonight?

Which sentence is an exclamatory sentence?

a.) Open your books.

b.) Where is your book?

c.) I can't find my book!

Sentences: Simple and Compound Sentences

Remember, a **simple sentence** is a sentence with only one **subject** and **predicate**.

Mary **bought a new dress.**

The children **are playing in the park.**

You **are very smart.**

You can join two simple sentences together to make a **compound sentence**. To do this you can use a comma (,) or a **conjunction**. There are over 100 conjunctions, also called transition words, the most common for creating compound sentences are these.

but	Contrasting information	I don't like tomatoes but I like ketchup.
so	Result or reason	I wanted an A so I studied for the test.
or	alternatives	I want red or pink ribbons.
and	addition	The dog is cute and smart.

Conjunction Practice: Use "and," "but," "or," and "so" to complete the sentences.

1. I want to eat pizza __________ spaghetti for dinner.
2. Sarah wants to play soccer __________ tennis this weekend.
3. He likes to read books __________ watch movies in his free time.
4. The weather is cold, __________ we're still going to the park.
5. Would you like chocolate __________ vanilla ice cream for dessert?
6. She studied hard, __________ she passed the test with flying colors.
7. He is allergic to peanuts, __________ he cannot eat peanut butter sandwiches.
8. We can go to the beach __________ visit the zoo tomorrow.

You can also use these conjunctions to put two simple sentences together.

Mary bought a new dress. She wore it to a party.

Mary bought a new dress and wore it to a party.

The children are playing in the park. It's going to rain soon.

The children are playing in the park but it's going to rain soon.

You are very smart. This will be very easy.

You are very smart so this will be very easy.

Sometimes a sentence can have a compound subject or predicate but that does not make it a compound sentence.

This sentence has a compound subject but is not a compound sentence.

Loretta is going to a movie. Alan is also going to a movie.

Loretta and Alan are going to a movie.

This sentence has a compound predicate but is not a compound sentence.

Midge likes comedy. Midge likes shopping.

Midge likes comedy and shopping.

Compound Sentence Practice

Read the sentence and decide if it is a compound or a simple sentence. Circle C if it is compound and S if it is simple.

1. I like ketchup but I don't like tomatoes.	C	S
2. My favorite food is pizza.	C	S
3. There are open seats in the front or you can stand in the back.	C	S
4. All the world's a stage.	C	S
5. Mint Chocolate is the worst ice cream flavor.	C	S

Use the given word and to make compound sentences.

1	**but**	The market is open on Sundays. It isn't open on holidays.
2	**and**	She likes BTS. She also likes the Beach Boys.
3	**or**	Do you want to go to a movie? Do you want to have dinner first?
4	**but**	I wanted to go to the concert. The tickets were sold out.
5	**so**	It's expensive to go to Europe. I saved for a year.

Run-On Sentences

You've learned that a compound sentence is two simple sentences that are put together with a comma (,) or a conjunction (and, but, or, so). However, when two sentences are put together without either of these or ending punctuation, this is called a run-on sentence.

Examples

I went to the store bought some cookies.
I went to college I studied French Literature.
There was a bad snowstorm school was canceled.
Lauren likes ketchup she doesn't like tomatoes.

There are two ways to fix a run-on sentence. The first way is to separate it into two sentences. Add an ending punctuation mark after the first sentence and capitalize the second sentence.

I went to the store. I bought some cookies.
I went to college. I studied French Literature.
There was a bad snowstorm. School was canceled.
Lauren likes ketchup. She doesn't like tomatoes.

Another way to fix a run-on sentence is to add a comma or conjunction to change it into a compound sentence.

I went to the store **and** bought some cookies.
I went to college **and** studied French Literature.
There was a bad snowstorm **so** school was canceled.
Lauren likes ketchup **but** she doesn't like tomatoes.

Practice: Each of the sentences below are run on sentences. Correct it first by separating it into two separate simple sentences. Then, correct it by adding a conjunction.

Example: Giraffes are vegetarians they don't eat meat.
Separate: Giraffes are vegetarians. They don't eat meat.
Conjunction: Giraffes are vegetarians so they don't eat meat.

1) Blue whales are the largest animals in the world very gentle.
Separate: ______________________________
Conj (and): ______________________________

2) Mosquitos are one of the smallest animals the most dangerous.
Separate: ______________________________
Conj (but): ______________________________

3) I have a pet rabbit I buy a lot of carrots.
Separate: ______________________________
Conj (so): ______________________________

4) Hamsters are tiny animals they make good pets.
Separate: ______________________________
Conj (so): ______________________________

Sentence Review:

Read the phrases below. If it is a complete sentence circle S, if it is a fragment circle F and if it is a run-on circle R.

I really like Mexican food.	S	F	R
Tacos are delicious.	S	F	R
I ate too much cake now I'm sick.	S	F	R
My mom makes great japchae.	S	F	R
I can't.	S	F	R
We have to clean my grandparents are coming.	S	F	R
My grandma's birthday.	S	F	R
I painted a picture for my grandma.	S	F	R
I painted her favorite flowers I hope she likes it.	S	F	R
I'll give it to her at the party.	S	F	R

Read the paragraph and fix the fragment and run on sentences. (3)

Yesterday, I went to the park with my friends. Played on the swings. Then, we had a picnic with sandwiches and juice. After that, we played soccer until it was time to go home. It was so much fun we saw a big rainbow in the sky. It was colorful and beautiful. We also found a caterpillar crawling on a leaf. I wanted to keep it as a pet my mom said we had to let it go. I hope we can go to the park again soon.

Put the words in the correct order to make a complete sentence.

very hot | It | is | .

____

the weather today | is | What | ?

____

Let's | ! | to the beach | go

____

forget | don't | to wear | ! | sunblock

____

swim | in the ocean | ? | Can you

____

sharks | ! | out for | Look

____

the best day ever | was | Today | !

____

Match the subject to the correct predicate and write the complete sentence on the lines.

My mother		are beautiful.
The children		makes us dinner every night.
I		want to be an astronaut.
My cat		is swimming in the lake.
A duck		are playing in the park.
The flowers		had kittens this weekend.

1. ______________________________

2. ______________________________

3. ______________________________

4. ______________________________

5. ______________________________

6. ______________________________

Read the sentence and circle the correct type of sentence. S for statement, C for command, Q for question, and E for exclamation.

1. Have you ever been to Rome?	S	C	Q	E
2. Everyone should go at least once.	S	C	Q	E
3. Beware of pickpockets!	S	C	Q	E
4. Rome is beautiful!	S	C	Q	E
5. The food is amazing.	S	C	Q	E
6. Millions of people visit Rome every year.	S	C	Q	E

Fix the run on sentence.

1. It's going to rain take an umbrella.

   ____

2. It may be expensive I want to go to New York.

   ____

3. My mom's birthday is tomorrow I need to buy flowers.

   ____

4. Marcia has a brother Jessica has a sister.

   ____

5. Spain is very laidback Italy is very busy.

   ____

Sentence Test

1. Identify the type of sentence: "The sun is shining brightly."
   a) Simple
   b) Compound
   c) Complex

2. Identify the type of sentence: "She likes to read books, and he enjoys playing soccer."
   a) Simple
   b) Compound
   c) Complex

3. Identify the type of sentence: "Although it was raining, they decided to go for a walk."
   a) Simple
   b) Compound
   c) Complex

4. Identify the type of sentence: "We studied for our exams because we wanted to do well."
   a) Simple
   b) Compound
   c) Complex

5. Choose the correct conjunction to complete the sentence: "I will go to the beach _____ it stops raining."
   a) and
   b) but
   c) until

6. Choose the correct conjunction to complete the sentence: "She couldn't sleep _____ she drank a cup of warm milk."
   a) so
   b) because
   c) although

7. Identify the sentence as a run-on sentence, a fragment, or correct: "The cat is sleeping it's raining outside."
   a) Run-on sentence
   b) Fragment
   c) Correct

8. Identify the sentence as a run-on sentence, a fragment, or correct: "After finishing his homework."
   a) Run-on sentence
   b) Fragment
   c) Correct

9. Identify the sentence as a run-on sentence, a fragment, or correct: "They played games at the park, the sun was shining."
   a) Run-on sentence
   b) Fragment
   c) Correct

10. Identify the sentence as a run-on sentence, a fragment, or correct: "Because she was tired and wanted to rest."
   a) Run-on sentence
   b) Fragment
   c) Correct

11. Correct the run-on sentence: "I want pizza I am hungry."

____

12. Correct the sentence fragment: "Running around the park."

____

13. Combine the following sentences to form a compound sentence:
"She loves to swim. He prefers to hike."

____

14. Combine the following sentences to form a complex sentence:
"The rain stopped. We went outside."

____

15. Identify the sentence type: "The dog barked, and the cat meowed."

____

16. Identify the sentence type: "Although it was late, they continued to work."

____

17. Identify the sentence type: "He likes to read books."

____

18. Identify the sentence type: "I enjoy watching movies, but I prefer reading."

____

19. Choose the correct conjunction to complete the sentence:
"She is tired _____ she has been working all day."
   a) and
   b) because
   c) so

20. Choose the correct conjunction to complete the sentence:
"I will go to the store _____ I need to buy some groceries."
   a) but
   b) because
   c) and

21. Correct the run-on sentence: "They played soccer the sun was shining."

____

22. Correct the sentence fragment: "After the storm passed."

____

23. Combine the following sentences to form a compound sentence:
"She enjoys painting. He likes to play the guitar."

____

24. Combine the following sentences to form a complex sentence:
"The birds chirped loudly. The sun rose in the sky."

____

25. Identify the sentence type: "She ran to catch the bus."

____

영어유치원 출신의 미국 거주 경험이 있는 G3 여학생

(Reading/ Writing : Weak, Speaking, Listening: Fluent)

- 어라운즈와 함께 한 준비기간: 3개월

이 학생은 어라운즈에서 3개월 정도 함께 준비한 학생입니다. 영어유치원 출신 및 미국에서 1년간 거주한 경험이 있는 학생이었기 때문에 발음과 리스닝은 부족하지 않았다는 강점을 가지고 있었습니다. 하지만 영어를 공부 보다는 생활 속에서 배운 학생이었기 때문에 단어를 외우는 능력이 부족하였고, 유창했던 스피킹과 리스닝 능력에 비해 리딩과 라이팅 부분에서는 아쉬운 부분이 있던 학생이었습니다.

- 어라운즈의 솔루션

부족했던 라이팅 및 단어 부분을 위해 선생님과 매일같이 라이팅 첨삭 및 분량채우기, 지속적인 단어 외우기를 했습니다. 리딩의 경우 타이머를 키고 제한 시간동안 빠르게 읽은 뒤, 메인 아이디어를 찾는 연습을 했습니다. 영어에 대해 이해가 있던 학생이었기 때문에 실력이 빠르게 늘었습니다. 그러나 한국식 영어공부에 적응하기까지 시간이 걸렸고, 특히 단어 외우는 것을 상당히 힘들어 했습니다. 학생의 성향을 관찰한 결과, 공부 습관을 들이게 도와주는 것이 우선 순위라고 판단되어 단톡방과 노트를 활용하여 어라운즈 선생님과 숙제를 꾸준히 공유하였습니다. 이런 꾸준한 관리로 학생은 공부 습관을 가질 수 있었고, 학생의 강점과 약점, 그리고 성향을 파악한 개인 맞춤 지도를 통해 불과 3개월이라는 시간동안 어라운즈와 함께 준비하여 제주 국제학교인 KIS 합격이라는 쾌거를 이루었습니다.

NOUNS

a.) Common & Proper Nouns
b.) Articles and Singular Nouns
c.) Plural Nouns
d.) Irregular Nouns
e.) Countable and Uncountable Nouns
f.) Possessive Nouns

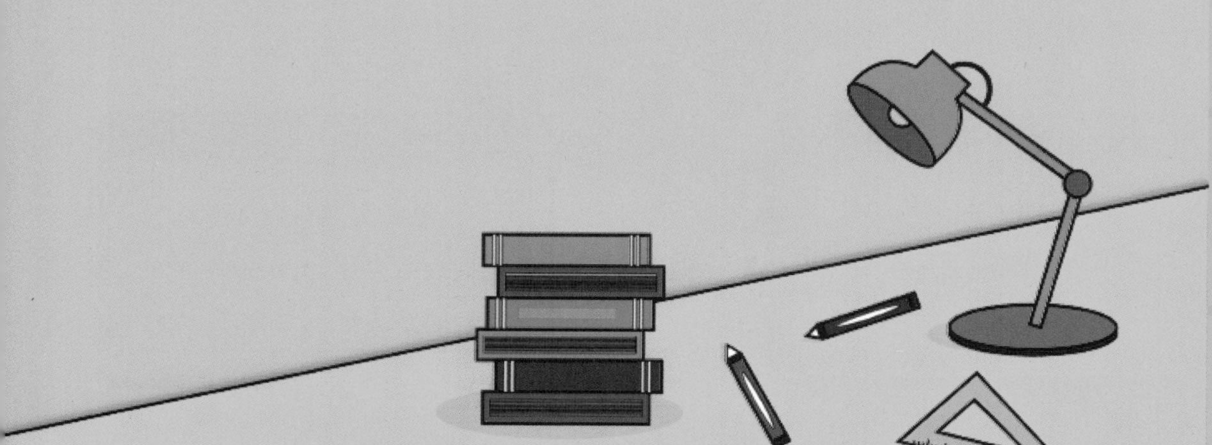

2. NOUNS

A **noun** is a word that tells the name of a person, place, thing, idea or animal.

person
mother
sister
teacher
player
lisa

place
mountains
ocean
store
school
street

thing
plant
desk
book
pencil
lamp

idea
love
strength
thought
friendship
happiness

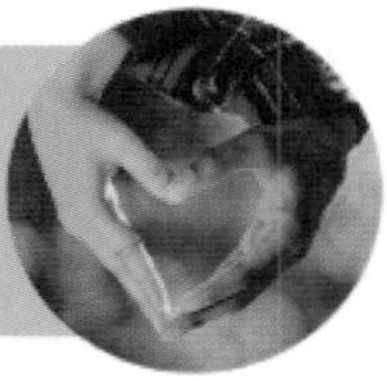

animal
bird
dog
cat
fish
lizard

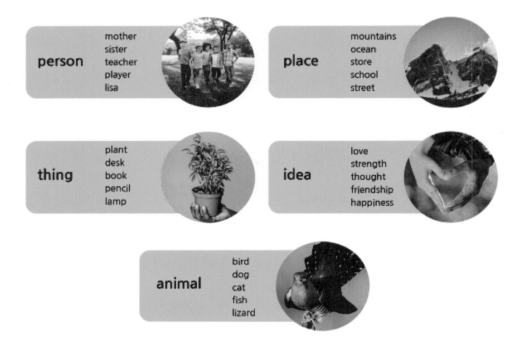

Practice: Write down 5 examples of a noun for each column.

Person	Place	Thing	Idea	Animal

Common noun VS Proper noun

A common noun tells the type of person, place or thing. Unless this noun is the first word in a sentence, it is going to start with a lowercase letter.

teacher **store** **cruise ship** **chimpanzee**

A proper noun gives the name of a person, place or thing. Think of it as being more important, so it needs a capital letter

Mrs. Kissel

Chi Chi
the Chimp

Cutler General
Store

Norwegian Jade

EXAMPLES

My **neighbor, Mary,** has a **cat** named **Mittens.**
In this sentence, neighbor, Mary, cat, and Mittens are all nouns.
The common nouns are neighbor (person) and cat (animal), the proper nouns are Mary (person's name) and Mittens (animal's name).

My **teacher, Mr. Johnson,** moved to **Korea** from **Toledo.**
In this sentence teacher, Mr. Johnson, Korea, and Toledo are all nouns.
Teacher (person) is a common noun. Mr. Johnson (person's name), Korea (place name), and Toledo (place name) are proper nouns.

I needed to go to the **store** to buy a **gift** for my **friend** so I went to **E-mart** and bought him a **PlayStation.**

In this sentence, the nouns are store, gift, friend, Emart, and Playstayion.
Store, gift, and friend are common nouns. Emart and PlayStation are proper nouns.

Practice: Read the story below. Circle the common nouns and underline the proper nouns.

My grandmother likes to visit her friend Margie.
She will go to her house and sit on the porch drinking lemonade.
Sometimes, they play games like Go Fish or Crazy Eights.
My grandmother takes her dog Mimi. Mimi is a Pomeranian.
She sits under my grandmother's chair sleeping. Grandma can't visit today
because Margie is in Mexico visiting her sister.

Practice: Complete the chart

Common	Proper Noun
school	Harvard
girl	
	Brian
store	
	McDonalds

Common Noun	Proper Noun
teacher	
	Baby Shark
movie	
	Coca Cola
book	

Capitalization Practice

Write the sentence correctly on the line. Make sure that all proper nouns have a capital letter.

1) my sister's name is angela.

____

2) one day, i want to visit the grand canyon.

____

3) we got burgers from mcdonalds.

____

4) my father is a professor at yale university.

____

5) i’ve been to disneyland in california, tokyo, and shanghai.

____

6) I’m going to the movies with francesca and marco on sunday.

____

Singular Nouns and Articles

You know that a noun is a person, place or thing, but they do not work alone. Nouns are always led by an article. This is a word that lets you know if this noun is special or ordinary. There are three articles.

A, an, and the

Use a or an if you are referring to one ordinary noun.

Example

an apple

a flower

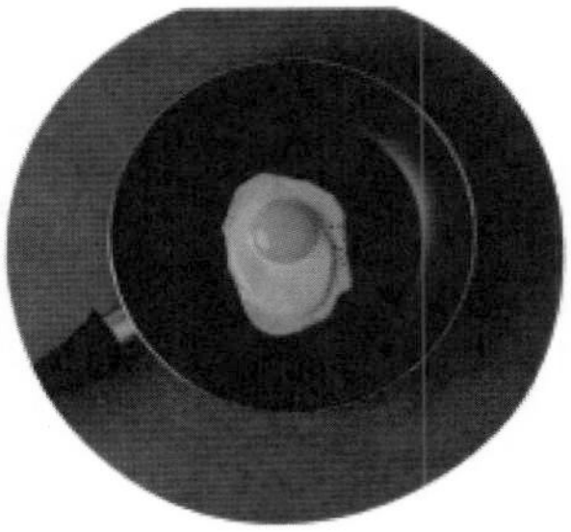

an egg in **a** skillet

an= the first letter of the noun is a vowel (a, e, i, o, or u)
a= the first letter is not a vowel

Practice: Read and circle a or an.

1.)	a / an	alien
2.)	a / an	cat
3.)	a / an	elephant
4.)	a / an	gold coin
5.)	a / an	ice cube
6.)	a / an	kangaroo

7.)	a / an	ball
8.)	a / an	dragon
9.)	a / an	fish
10.)	a / an	hero
11.)	a / an	juice box
12.)	a / an	lion

Use "the" if you are referring to a specific or special noun, or more than one

The apples on the tree

The moon

The teacher
The students

Practice: Read the sentence, fill in the blank with **a**, **an**, or **the**

1. Do you want to go to ________ zoo this weekend?
2. Sure, but is there ____________ panda habitat?
3. Yes, but ________ pandas are usually hiding.
4. I wanted to take _________ picture with them.
5. You can take a picture with ___________elephant.
6. I'm afraid of __________ elephants!
7. My teacher volunteered at ________ sanctuary for elephants in Thailand.
8. She said ________ volunteers had a lot of fun.
9. She even fed one elephant __________ banana.

Plural Nouns

You know that a noun is a person, place, thing, idea, or animal and that you need to use an article a or an if the noun is **singular**, or only one.

A girl is petting **an elephant**

A boy is carrying **an umbrella**

A statue sits by **a pond**

Use "the" if the noun is special or specific. You can also use "the" if it is a plural noun (more than one person, place, thing, idea, or animal)

The presents are under the tree

The bird is eating **the berries**

The students are in **the library**

To make a singular noun a plural noun just add -s to the end of it.
If a singular noun ends in **-s**, **-ch**, **-sh**, **-x**, or **-z**, then add **-es** to make it plural.

Practice: look and write -s or -es to make the singular noun plural.

Ex. Girl s

1. computer___
2. bush___
3. cart___
4. fox___
5. bench___

Ex. Box es

1. toy___
2. bottle___
3. chicken___
4. shoe___
5. glass___

There are two other endings that you should be mindful of.
If a singular noun ends with **consonant-y,** then the y changes to an i and then add -es.

If a singular noun ends in **-f** or **-fe**, change the **-f** or **-fe** to a v and add **-es** to make it plural.

berries

ladies

shelves

leaves

Practice: Complete the sentence with the correct form of the word.

1. [berry] I had a cup of mixed __________ with lunch.
2. [shelf] Put the book on the __________.
3. [elf] Have you ever wondered how Santa found the __________.
4. [city] Did you visit many __________ in Italy?

Irregular Nouns

There are some nouns that change their spelling completely to show more than one. These are called irregular nouns.

Singular	Plural	Singular	Plural	Singular	Plural
person	people	goose	geese	mouse	mice
tooth	teeth	ox	oxen	deer	deer
child	children	foot	feet	woman	women
fish	fish	sheep	sheep	fungus	fungi
cactus	cacti	man	men	wolf	wolves

Practice: Look and write.

Countable and Uncountable Nouns

You know that a noun is a person, place, thing, animal, or idea. If there is only one noun it is called a singular noun and if there is more than one it is a plural noun. Most nouns have an ending based on the last letter of the word. Some do not change at all. These are called non-countable nouns.

A non-countable noun is something that cannot be separated as a single thing, it is a smaller part of a larger thing.

Countable		Non-Countable	
sandwiches	flowers	water	trash
apples	bananas	cereal	spaghetti
oxen	computers	butter	rice
movies	books	cheese	jam

Practice: Choose the correct word to complete the sentence.

1. We had **spaghetti | spaghettis** for dinner.
2. There are **monkey | monkeys** in the trees.
3. We volunteered to pick up **trash | trashes** this weekend.
4. I have to take these **book | books** back to the library.
5. I like Four **Cheese | Cheeses** pizza.
6. May we have three **hamburger | hamburgers**, please?
7. We drank some orange **juice | juices** after the game.
8. There are **oxes | oxen** in the field.
9. I will make some **rice | rices** for dinner.

Uncountable Nouns and Articles: Remember that common nouns are always led by an article. Uncountable nouns typically use some or any as their article.

a	an	the	some	any
Singular nouns starting with a consonant	Singular nouns starting with a vowel	Plural nouns	-Uncountable nouns (positive sentences) -questions	-Uncountable nouns (negative sentence) -questions

Count/Noncount Nouns and Articles Practice: Write the correct article (a, an, the, some, any) to complete the sentence.

1. There is ________ sandwich on the table.
2. There are __________ bananas in the bag.
3. May I have __________ juice?
4. There aren't ________ olives in the salad.
5. Is there _________ salad on the menu?
6. I need _________ pencil.
7. There's _________ elephant in my pajamas.
8. Keep an eye on _________ clock.
9. Do you want to see __________ movie.
10. I really need ___________ coffee.

Possessive Noun

When you want to show that a noun has or owns something that is a **possessive noun**.
To turn a common noun into a possessive noun add an apostrophe and -s to the end of it.

This book **belongs to Mike**. → This is **Mike's** book.
The **name of the cat** is Spot. → The **cat's** name is Spot.

If the noun is plural there will likely already be an s at the end. In these cases you don't have to add an additional s, only the apostrophe.

This room is **for the editors**. → This is the **editors'** room.
These pants are **for boys**. → These are **boys'** pants.

However, if the noun is an irregular noun and the plural form does not have an s at the end, then add 's to the end as normal.

These shoes are **for women**. → These are **women's** shoes.
The cage is **for the mice**. → This is the **mice's** cage.

Possessive Noun Practice: Write the noun in the possessive form.

1) Michael

____

2) The dog

____

3) The girls

____

1) Jason

____

2) Teacher

____

3) Lisa

____

Complete the sentence with the possessive noun.

1. [Marsha] The ball hit _______________ nose.
2. [the cows] We cleaned the _____________ stalls.
3. [gardener] You'll find a rake in the ____________ shed.
4. [batter] Baez is practicing in the ______________ cage.
5. [Jennie] Have you heard ______________ new song?
6. [mom] I really miss my ____________ cooking.
7. [girls] These are __________ shoes.
8. [fly] The boy plucked the ____________wings.
9. [sister] I helped curl my ___________ hair for the party.
10. [Greg] That is ____________ bike.

Read the sentence, if there is a mistake, circle it and write the correction on the line. If it is correct, write "correct".

11. Have you seen the baby's clothes? ________________
12. I need to borrow Michaels' computer. ________________
13. These are the boys' jeans. ________________
14. Turn off the lightes before bed. ________________
15. I`m looking for my dads glasses. ________________
16. These are cat's toys. ________________

Noun Review:

Circle the nouns in the paragraph.

Once upon a time there was a beautiful princess, named Cinderella. She lived with her stepmother and two sisters. They were not kind to Cinderella and made her clean the ashes, which is how she got her name. One day a kind fairy helped to send her to a ball held by the king and queen to help their son find a wife. Prince Christopher fell in love with Cinderella right away. They were married and lived happily ever after.

Read the sentence. If there is a mistake, circle it and make the correction on the line. If the sentence is correct, write "Correct" on the line.

17. My name is marsha brady. ________________
18. Tiffany went to harvard University. ________________
19. I want Burger King for dinner. ________________
20. The panda had two babys. ________________
21. I had an sandwich for lunch. ________________
22. There are a lot of people here. ________________
23. There aren't any childrens in the park. ________________
24. She has an apple computer. ________________

Nouns Test

1. Identify the proper noun:
"The dog chased the cat up the tree."
   a) dog
   b) cat
   c) tree

2. Identify the common noun: "We visited the Grand Canyon last summer."
   a) Grand Canyon
   b) summer
   c) visited

3. Choose the plural form of the noun: "book"
   a) books
   b) book's
   c) books'

4. Choose the singular form of the noun: "mice"
   a) mouse
   b) mouses
   c) mice's

5. Choose the correct article for the noun: "_ apple fell from the tree."
   a) An
   b) A
   c) The

6. Choose the correct article for the noun: "_ oranges are my favorite fruit."
   a) An
   b) A
   c) The

7. Identify the uncountable noun: "The teacher gave us some advice before the exam."
   a) teacher
   b) exam
   c) advice

8. Identify the countable noun:
"There are three cars parked in the driveway."
   a) three
   b) driveway
   c) cars

9. Choose the possessive form of the noun: "dog"
   a) dogs'
   b) dog's
   c) dogs's

10. Choose the possessive form of the noun: "children"
   a) child
   b) children's
   c) childs'

11. Choose the plural form of the noun: "knife"
   a) knifes
   b) knive
   c) knives

12. Choose the singular form of the noun: "people"
a) person
b) peoples
c) people's

13. Identify the common noun: "The Statue of Liberty stands in New York Harbor."
a) Statue of Liberty
b) New York Harbor
c) stands

14. Identify the proper noun: "The boys played soccer in the park."
a) boys
b) soccer
c) park

15. Choose the correct article for the noun: "_ elephant is the largest land mammal."
a) An
b) A
c) The

16. Choose the correct article for the noun: "_ ocean covers more than 70% of the Earth's surface."
a) An
b) A
c) The

17. Identify the uncountable noun: "She bought some milk from the store."
a) bought
b) store
c) milk

18. Identify the countable noun: "There are many clouds in the sky."
a) many
b) sky
c) clouds

19. Choose the possessive form of the noun: "cat"
a) cats
b) cats's
c) cat's

20. Choose the possessive form of the noun: "teacher"
a) teachers'
b) teacher's
c) teachers's

21. Choose the plural form of the noun: "box"
a) box
b) boxs
c) boxes

22. Choose the singular form of the noun: "toys"
a) toy's
b) toys's
c) toy

23. Identify the common noun: "The Eiffel Tower is located in Paris."
a) Eiffel Tower
b) Paris
c) located

24. Identify the proper noun: "The students studied geography in school."

a) students
b) geography
c) school

25. Choose the correct article for the noun: "_ apple a day keeps the doctor away."

a) An
b) A
c) The

영어유치원 출신의 G3 남학생

(Reading/ Writing : Fluent -Speaking, Listening: Fluent)

- 어라운즈와 함께 준비한 기간: 2개월

이 학생은 모든 것이 완벽했습니다. 그러나 스스로 생각하고 답을 찾아가는 창의적인 수업 방식을 채택하는 국제학교의 성격과는 달리, 외운듯한 대답을 반복하는 창의력이 부족한 학생이었습니다. 마치 라이팅의 경우, G3학생이 스스로 생각하여 쓴 문장이라기 보다는 예상 답변을 미리 외워 그대로 쓴 듯한 부자연스러움이 있었습니다.
또한 스피킹의 경우도 마찬가지로 학생의 주관이나 개인적인 특성을 뚜렷하게 파악할 수 없는 외운듯한 답변이 돌아왔습니다.

- 어라운즈의 솔루션

이 학생의 경우, 실력은 완벽했지만 위와 같은 부분들로 인해 굉장히 어려운 케이스였습니다.
기본기가 아닌 테크닉에만 신경을 써서 쌓은 실력을 온전히 학생의 실력으로 만들기 위해서는 처음부터 다시 시작해야 했기 때문입니다. 이러한 상황에서 학생은 맵테스트 200점에서 더 이상 발전이 없었습니다. 어라운즈는 학생의 성향을 파악한 후 처음부터 다시 꼼꼼하게 기본기를 쌓아가는 것부터 시작했습니다. 단어나 문제 위주의 공부 보다는 학생이 스스로 생각하는 바를 표현할 수 있도록 만드는 데 집중하였습니다. 창의적으로 생각할 수 있도록 만들어 주었고 학생은 NLCS에 합격하였습니다. 자신감을 학생이 가질 수 있었고 인터뷰를 할 때 모르는 단어가 나와도 오히려 선생님께 물어보면서 당황하지 않는 것 또한 어라운즈에서 배웠습니다. 모르는 부분이 나와도 당황해서 말을 못하는 것이 아닌 위기 대처 능력 또한 배웠습니다.

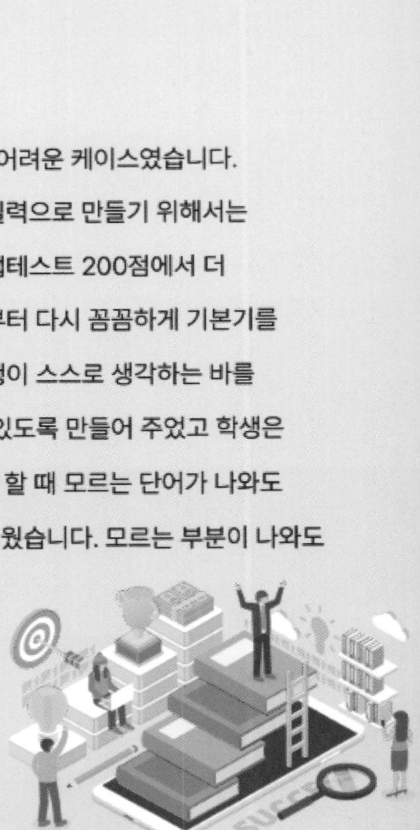

PRONOUNS

a.) Subject Pronouns
b.) Object Pronouns
c.) Possessive Pronouns
d.) Relative Pronouns
e.) Reflexive Pronouns

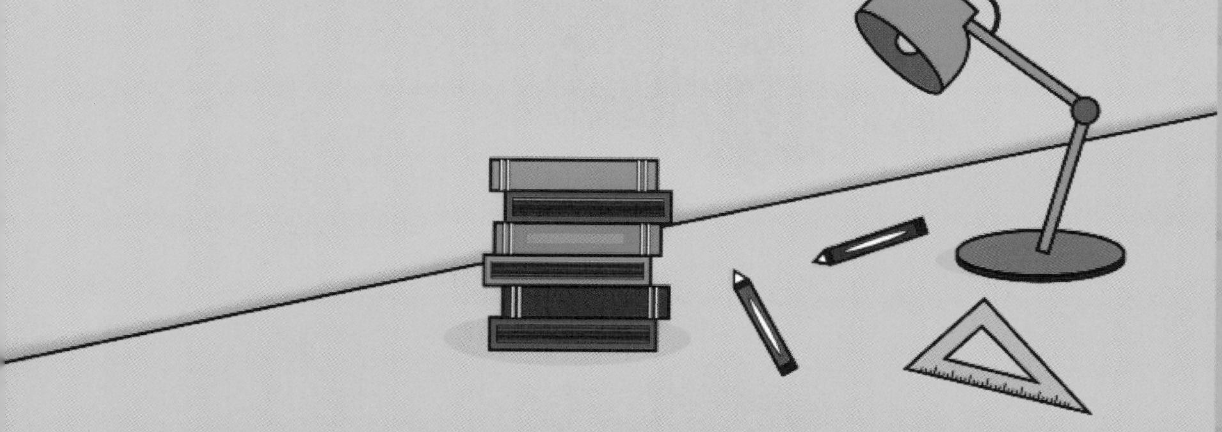

3. PRONOUN

Read the story below. Circle all of the nouns.

Michael is excited. Michael is going to Michael's grandmother's house this weekend. Michael's grandmother lives on a farm. Michael is very excited to feed the cows and chickens. Michael will also go fishing with Michael's grandfather. If Michael and Michael's grandfather catch a fish, Michael's grandmother will cook the fish for dinner. Michael, Michael's grandmother, and Michael's grandmother can't wait for Michael's visit.

How many times is Michael's name written? ________

Instead of writing the same noun over and over again we use pronouns.
A pronoun is a word that takes the place of a noun.

Look at the first two sentences again:

Michael is excited. ~~Michael~~ He is going to Michael's grandmother's house this weekend.

"He" is a pronoun that took the place of the noun "Michael".

He is going to Michael's grandmother's house this weekend. ~~Michael's grandmother~~ she lives on a farm.

This time we replaced Michael's grandmother with she.

Michael will also go fishing with Michael's grandfather. If ~~Michael and Michael's grandfather~~ they catch a fish. Michael's grandmother will cook ~~the fish~~ it for dinner.

Subject Pronouns

The story is much easier to read now thanks to pronouns.

Michael is excited. **He** is going to his grandmother's house this weekend. **She** lives on a farm. Michael is very excited to feed the cows and chickens. **He** will also go fishing his grandfather. If they catch a fish, Michael's grandmother will cook it for dinner. **They** can't wait for his visit.

Notice all of these pronouns happened in the subject of the sentence, these are called subject pronouns.

Subject Pronouns						
Singular					Plural	
I	you	he	she	it	we	they

Pronoun Practice: Read the story and replace the highlighted nouns with the correct subject pronoun.

Jasmine wanted to go to the party. The party was for Brian's birthday. Brian[1] would have chocolate cake. Jasmine[2] wanted to find the perfect present for Brian. Jasmine went to three stores before Jasmine[3] found one. Brian loved dinosaurs. Brian[4] would like the dinosaur game that Jasmine found. The game had a dinosaur theme. Maybe Jasmine and Brian[5] could play the game[6] together.

1)	2)	3)
4)	5)	6)

Object Pronouns

Remember that a sentence can be broken down into three parts.

Practice: Read the sentences. Circle the subjects and underline the object.

1. She likes ice cream.
2. He went to the store.
3. We are going on a picnic.
4. I recently read **The Hobbit.**
5. It is cold outside.
6. Are you hungry?
7. They are watching a movie.

When you are replacing a noun that is acting as the object of the sentence, use an object pronoun.

Object Pronouns						
Singular					Plural	
me	you	him	her	it	us	them

Practice: Write the correct object pronoun and circle the subject noun it replaces.

8. I really like cookies. I could eat _______ everyday.
9. Jack chased Jill up the hill. She chased ________ after.
10. There is a cake on the table. Please don't touch ________.
11. Lauren is on the phone. Do you want to talk to _______.
12. I got a gold medal yesterday. My school gave it to ______.

Subject and Object Pronoun Review:

Complete the sentence with the correct pronoun.

1. ______ like coffee and tea.
2. ________ is the girl in the blue dress.
3. Do ________ like to go hiking?
4. _______ asked his mom to give him ice cream.
5. _______ are going to the movies after dinner.
6. Can you bring those books to ________.
7. Maria's brother picks ______ up from school everyday.
8. My brother loves the video game I gave _______.
9. Our teacher is going to tell ______ who won the science competition.

Choose the correct sentence.

1.

a.) Tree climb you?

b.) Can you climb a tree?

2.

a.) We all have iPhones except she.

b.) We all have iPhones except her.

3.

a.) Us had a picnic in the park?

b.) We had a picnic in the park?

4.

a.) He has a big test tomorrow.

b.) Him has a big test tomorrow.

5.

a.) Her is going to Spain this year.

b.) She is going to Spain this year.

Possessive pronouns

Possessive pronouns are pronouns that show that something belongs to someone.

Possessive Pronouns						
Singular					Plural	
mine	yours	his	hers		ours	theirs

Practice: Fill in the blank with the correct possessive pronoun.

Ex. I bought these cookies. They are ___________.

1. Peter and Mary got new bikes. These are ___________.
2. I don't have a pen, can I borrow ___________.
3. This shirt belongs to John. It is ___________.
4. Jessica let me borrow a cup, this is ___________.
5. We just got a new car. The blue one is ___________.
6. If these are your shoes, where are ___________?

Read the sentence. If there is a mistake, circle it and make the correction on the line. If the sentence is correct, write "Correct" on the line.

1. Come to our house for dinner. ___________
2. My sister lives in Spain? ___________
3. Is this you pencil? ___________

Relative Pronoun

A relative pronoun is a pronoun that is used to introduce a relative clause that gives more information about the noun that comes before this pronoun.
The most common pronouns are who, whom, whose, which, and that.

The man **who lives upstairs** plays the piano all the time.

Chance, **whom** you are sitting next to, auditioned for American Idol.

Mary, **whose** mom is a chef, can't cook.

I will go to the BTS concert, **which** is next year.

These are the shoes **that** she wore in the movie.

Relative Pronoun Practice: Circle the relative pronouns in the sentence in sentence.

1. Can you pass me the cup that's on the table?
2. I'm the one who made the cake.
3. I found a dress which I love!
4. Let's go someplace where we've never been before!
5. You can invite whomever you like to the party.

Reflexive pronouns

Reflexive Pronouns are pronouns that end in -self or -selves, and refer back to the subject of the sentence.

Possessive Pronouns						
Singular					Plural	
myself	yourself	himself	herself	itself	ourselves	themselves

I treated **myself** to some ice cream.

Are you traveling by **yourself**?

He fell and hurt **himself**.

She bought **herself** a new dress.

A cat can clean **itself**.

We sat and talked to **ourselves**.

They can entertain **themselves.**

Can you finish it **yourselves**?

Reflexive Pronoun Practice: Choose the sentence that is written correctly.

1.)	Help yourself to some popcorn.	Help youself to some popcorn.	Help you to some popcorn.
2.)	The baby can feed hiself.	The baby can feed himself.	The baby can feed heself.
3.)	I made my dress meself.	I made my dress myself.	I made my dress Iself.
4.)	She can buy flowers for herself.	She can buy flowers for sheself.	She can buy flowers himself.
5.)	We can seat ourselves.	We can seat ourselfs.	We can seat usselves.

Read the sentence. If there is a mistake, circle it and make the correction on the line. If the sentence is correct, write "Correct" on the line.

1. I can move the couch myself. ____________________
2. She's not afraid to travel by himself. ____________________
3. Dad made dinner himself. ____________________
4. Cats lick itself clean. ____________________
5. The horse can get home itself. ____________________
6. He put myself through school. ____________________
7. I'm too tired to cook dinner for herself. ____________________
8. They locked themselves out of the house. ____________________

Pronoun Review:

Read the paragraph and circle the pronouns.

Once, two kids, Alex and Emily, got stuck in a candy store. They looked everywhere but couldn't find a way out. They felt hungry and scared. Then, the store owner came back, unlocked the door, and let them go. They were happy to be free again after their candy store adventure. They promised to be more careful next time they went exploring.

Fill in the blank with the correct pronoun.

1. ________ went to the store to buy some apples.
2. She gave ________ a present for his birthday.
3. The book ________ is reading is very interesting.
4. That's John, ________ is the tallest student in the class.
5. I saw a movie by ________ last night.
6. The teacher asked ________ to turn in their homework.
7. They couldn't find ________ keys.
8. The dog ________ barks loudly, chased the cat up a tree.
9. Sarah, ________ is my best friend, invited me to her birthday party.
10. The children ________ built the sandcastle at the beach were proud of their creation.

Read the sentence, circle any mistakes and write the correction on the line.

1. Him went to the store to buy some candy. ________________
2. She gave me a present for his birthday. ________________
3. The book her is reading is very interesting. ________________
4. Him is the tallest student in the class. ________________
5. I saw a movie with she last night. ________________

Choose the correct sentence.

1.)	Her went to the park with his friends.	She went to the park with his friends.	She went to the park with her friends.
2.)	Me loves to play with he at recess.	I loves to play with him at recess.	I love to play with him at recess.
3.)	Him ate all of the cookies by he.	He ate all of the cookies by him.	He ate off of the cookies by himself.
4.)	They picked up she after school.	Them picked up her after school.	They picked her up after school.
5.)	We made a card for they.	US made a card for them.	We made a card for them.

Pronoun Test

Subject Pronouns

1. Choose the correct subject pronoun to complete the sentence: _____ went to the park with his friends.

a.) her
b.) she
c.) he
d.) him

2. Fill in the blank with the correct subject pronoun: _____ like to play soccer after school.

We
b.) Us
c.) Them
d.) They

3. Which word is the subject pronoun in the sentence: "_____ will read the book tomorrow"?

a.) Book
b.) Read
c.) Tomorrow
d.) They

4. Select the subject pronoun: _____ ate all the pizza by himself.

a.) He
b.) Him
c.) His
d.) Her

5. Choose the correct subject pronoun: _____ and Sarah are best friends.

a.) Him
b.) They
c.) Her
d.) She

Object Pronouns

6. Which word is the object pronoun in the sentence: "She gave _____ a gift"?

a.) She
b.) Gave
c.) Her
d.) They

7. Fill in the blank with the correct object pronoun: Mom asked _____ to help with the dishes.

a.) He
b.) Her
c.) Them
d.) They

8. Choose the correct object pronoun to complete the sentence: She gave the ball to _____.

a.) We
b.) Us
c.) They
d.) Him

9. Select the object pronoun: The teacher asked _____ to read aloud.
a.) He
b.) Him
c.) His
d.) They

10. Fill in the blank with the correct object pronoun: Can you help _____ with the puzzle?
a.) She
b.) Her
c.) They
d.) Them

Reflexive Pronouns

11. Which word is the reflexive pronoun in the sentence:
"He washed _____ before dinner"?
a.) He
b.) Washed
c.) His
d.) Himself

12. Fill in the blank with the correct reflexive pronoun: Sarah can tie her shoes by _____.
a.) She
b.) Her
c.) Herself
d.) They

13. Select the reflexive pronoun:
He made breakfast for _____.
a.) He
b.) Him
c.) His
d.) HImself

14. Choose the correct reflexive pronoun to complete the sentence:
They taught _____ how to ride a bike.
a.) They
b.) Them
c.) Themselves
d.) Theirs

15. Fill in the blank with the correct reflexive pronoun: Did you make this card by _____?
a.) She
b.) Her
c.) Yourself
d.) Themselves

16. Choose the correct pronoun to complete the sentence: _____ is my sister.
a.) Her
b.) She
c.) They
d.) Their

17. Fill in the blank with the correct pronoun: He gave _____ a high five.
a.) Her
b.) She
c.) They
d.) Them

18. Select the pronoun: Can _____ come to the party too?
a.) She
b.) He
c.) Them
d.) They

19. Choose the correct pronoun: We went to the zoo and saw _____ favorite animals.
a.) Them
b.) They
c.) Their
d.) Our

20. Fill in the blank with the correct pronoun: Did you enjoy _____ at the park yesterday?
a.) She
b.) Them
c.) We
d.) Us

일반 한국 초등학교 출신의 G3 남학생

(Reading, Writing, Speaking, Listening: Weak)

- 어라운즈와 함께 준비한 기간: 2개월

이 학생의 경우 모든 영역이 약했습니다. 하지만 이 학생에게는 굉장히 유리한 강점이 있었습니다. 바로, 의욕과 자신감이 남달랐고 숙제를 상당히 잘 해오는 등 의지가 강했습니다.
모든 영역이 약했지만 스스로 성장하고자 하는 욕심이 강했기 때문에 이러한 성향을 파악하고 나니,2개월 이라는 시간 동안 학생에게 최상의 결과를 줄 수 있는 커리큘럼을 짤 수 있었습니다.

- 어라운즈의 솔루션

모든 영역을 공부해야 하는 만큼, 그리고 2달이라는 짧은 시간이 남은 만큼 리스크가 컸습니다. 하지만 학생의 의욕이 넘쳤고, 그에 맞게 구성한 어라운즈의 커리큘럼으로 학생의 실력을 향상시켰습니다. 2달 동안 상당히 많은 양의 리딩을 하고, 읽은 것들을 요약하며 리딩에 대한 기본기를 다지는 것과 동시에 학생 스스로 생각하며 요약할 수 있는 창의성 또한 길렀습니다. 꾸준히 일기를 쓰는 것부터 시작으로 스스로의 생각을 글로 피력할 수 있게 되었으며 이후에는 에세이 라이팅까지 가능할 정도의 실력을 쌓았습니다. 특히 스피킹의 경우, 예상 답변을 외우는 것이 아닌 스스로의 생각을 말 할수 있는 능력을 향상시키는 데 집중하였습니다. 그 결과, 학생은 당당히 KIS에 합격하였습니다.

Verbs

a.) Be Verbs
b.) Present Tense
c.) Present Simple Irregular Verbs
d.) Present Progressive
e.) Irregular Present Continuous
f.) Past Tense
g.) Past Tense Irregular
h.) Present Simple vs Past Simple
i.) Future Tense
j.) Modal Verbs
k.) Perfect Tense
l.) Subject Verb Agreement

4. VERBS

Remember that sentences come in three parts.

SUBJECT | VERB | OBJECT

Verbs are the action words in a sentence. They show what the subject does.

Jackie | **brushed** | **the horse.**

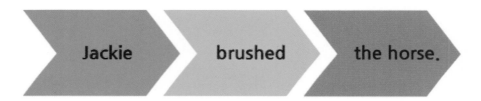

"Jackie" is the subject of the sentence. The action that she is performing is "brush". The object being brushed is "the horse".

My grandparents | go | dancing on the weekend.

"My grandparents" are the subjects of the sentence. The action they perform is to "go". The object, the place the go, is "dancing on the weekend".

Practice: Draw a square around the verb.

1. The cat sleeps peacefully on the windowsill.
2. Sarah dances ballet every Saturday.
3. The sun shines brightly in the sky.
4. Max runs quickly in the race.
5. The birds sing sweetly in the morning.

Practice: Put the sentence in order.

1. jumps / the / happily / dog / up / and / down

____

2. in / the / my / park / friends / play / and / I

____

3. eats / the / lunch / squirrel / in / the / tree

____

4. sings / the / sweetly / bird / morning / in / the

____

Be verbs

Be verbs are verbs that show that something exists, has happened or describes its characteristics.

Be verbs						
Am	Is			Are		
I	he	she	it	we	they	you

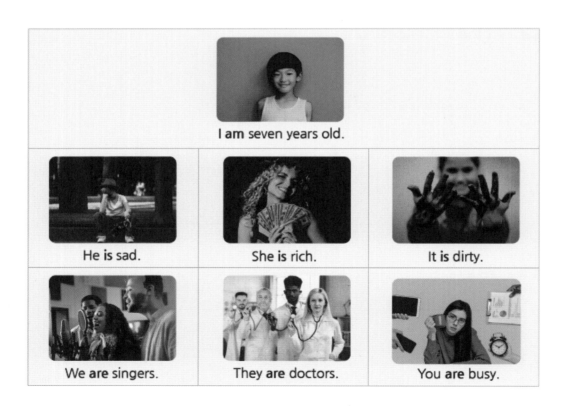

I **am** seven years old.

He **is** sad.

She **is** rich.

It **is** dirty.

We **are** singers.

They **are** doctors.

You **are** busy.

Negative Be Verbs

To show that something doesn't exist, happen, or that something doesn't have a particular characteristic, put not after the verb: am not, is not, or are not.

These phrases are typically shortened into contractions.
To make a negative verb contraction, take out the space and substitute the "o" in "not" with an apostrophe. Note: am no cannot be shortened.

I'm **not** seven years old.

He **isn't** happy.

She **isn't** poor.

It **isn't** clean.

We **aren't** dancers.

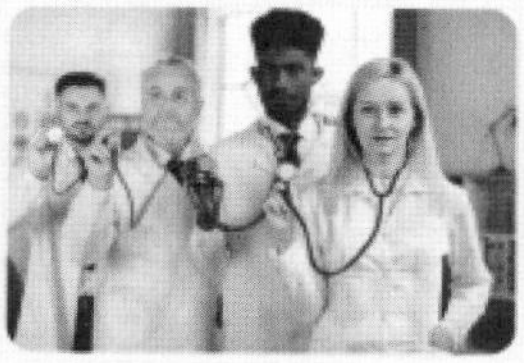

They **aren't** teachers.

You **aren't** free.

Be Verbs Practice: Fill in the blank with the correct be verb.

1. Sarah __________ happy when she plays with her friends.

2. The sky __________ blue on a sunny day.

3. My cat __________ sleeping on the couch.

4. The flowers __________ blooming in the garden.

5. The book __________ interesting to read.

6. The dog __________ barking at the mailman.

7. My mom __________ cooking dinner in the kitchen.

8. The stars __________ shining brightly in the night sky.

9. The baby __________ laughing and giggling.

10. Our teacher __________ kind and helpful to us.

Present Tense

Verbs have many different forms of tenses. Present tense verbs show things that are routine or that actions happening now.

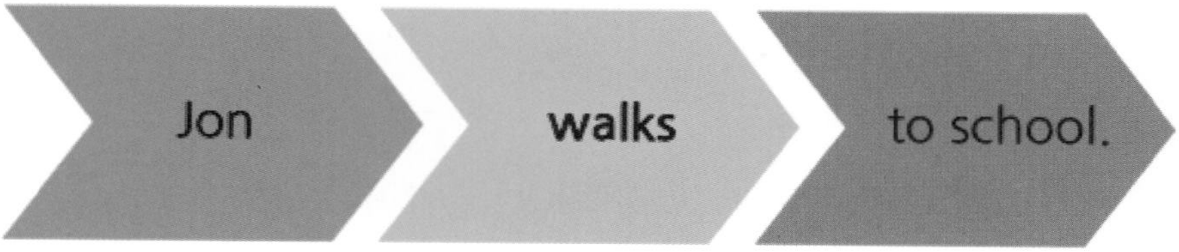

Regular present tense verbs take the verb and will add a form of "s" to the end of it, depending on the number of nouns in the subject. SIngular subjects **he, she, and it** will have an "s" added to the end. **I, you**, and plural subjects including **we** and **they** will not have an "s".

Verbs ending in a consonant, add an "s"

Regular Present Simple Verbs (walk)						
Singular					Plural	
I walk.	You walk.	He walks.	She walks.	It walks.	We walk.	They walk.

Verbs ending in ch, sh, s, or x, add "es".

Regular Present Simple Verbs (push)						
Singular					Plural	
I push.	You push.	He pushes.	She pushes.	It pushes.	We push.	They push.

Verbs that end with a consonant + y add "ies".

Regular Present Simple Verbs (cry)						
Singular					Plural	
I cry.	You cry.	He cries.	She cries.	It cries.	We cry.	They cry.

Present Simple Practice: Complete the sentence with the provided verb correctly.

1. Sarah ___________ (play) soccer with her friends after school.
2. The birds ___________ (sing) beautifully in the trees every morning.
3. My mom ___________ (cook) dinner for our family in the evening.
4. The sun ___________ (shine) brightly in the sky during the day.
5. Max and Emily ___________ (study) together for their math test.
6. The cat ___________ (sleep) peacefully on the windowsill.
7. We ___________ (visit) Grandma and Grandpa on Sundays.
8. The flowers ___________ (bloom) in the garden during the spring.
9. Dad ___________ (drive) us to school every morning.
10. The teacher ___________ (teach) us new lessons every day.
11. Alex ___________ (read) his favorite book before bedtime.
12. The dog ________ (bark) loudly whenever someone knocks on the door.

Read the sentence. If there is a mistake, circle it and make the correction on the line. If the sentence is correct, write "Correct" on the line.

1. Sarah play soccer after school. ________________
2. The birds sing every morning. ________________
3. My mom cooking dinner for our family in the evening. ________________
4. The sun shines brightly in the sky during the night. ________________

Present Simple Irregular Verbs

Irregular Present Simple Verbs (do)						
Singular					Plural	
I do.	You do.	He does.	She does.	It does.	We do.	They do.

Irregular Present SImple Verbs (go)						
Singular					Plural	
I go.	You go.	He goes.	She goes.	It goes.	We go.	They go.

Irregular Present Simple Verbs (have)						
Singular					Plural	
I have.	You have.	He has.	She has.	It has.	We have.	They have.

Present Simple Irregular Practice: Fill in the blank with the correct usage of the given verb.

1. Sarah ________ (do) her homework every day after school.
2. Max and Emily __________ (go) to the park on weekends.
3. The cat __________ (take) a nap in the afternoon sun.
4. We __________ (have) pizza for dinner on Fridays.
5. Mom ___________ (go) to work early in the morning.

Write about your daily routine. What are some things that you do every day? Where do you do them and who do you do them with? T
ry to have at least 7-10 sentences and make sure that you practice using present simple verbs correctly.

Present Progressive

Present Progressive or Present Continuous are verbs that are happening right now and will eventually stop. To show what you are currently doing you use a be verb + verb + ing.

Jon | **is walking** | to school.

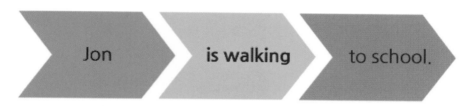

Present Continuous Verbs (sleep)						
Singular					Plural	
I am sleeping.	You are sleeping.	He is sleeping	She is sleeping.	It is sleeping.	We are sleeping.	They are sleeping.

If the verb ends in a consonant + a vowel + consonant, double the last consonant and "ing".

Present Continuous Verbs (run)						
Singular					Plural	
I am running.	You are running.	He is running.	She is running.	It is running.	We are running.	They are running.

If the verb ends with a consonant and an e, drop the e before adding "ing".

Irregular Present Continuous Verbs (come)						
Singular					Plural	
I am coming.	You are coming.	He is coming.	She is coming.	It is coming.	We are coming.	They are coming.

Irregular Present Continuous Practice: Write the word correctly in Present Progressive tense.

1. Swim:	________	9. Write:	________
2. Run:	________	10. Sing:	________
3. Play:	________	11. Paint:	________
4. Dance:	________	12. Laugh:	________
5. Read:	________	13. Study:	________
6. Jump:	________	14. Talk:	________
7. Sleep:	________	15. Cook:	________
8. Eat:	________	16. Climb:	________

Present Progressive Practice: Choose the correct word from the word bank to complete the sentence using present progressive tense.

play	run	laugh
eat	sleep	jump

1. Sarah ________________ with her friends at the playground.
2. The dog ________________ in the backyard.
3. Max and Emily ________________ in the park.
4. The cat ________________ on the windowsill.
5. We ________________ pizza for dinner tonight.
6. The children ________________ and having fun at the party.

Present Continuous Review:

Read the sentence, if there are any mistakes, circle it and write the correction on the line. If it is correct, write "Correct" on the line.

1. Sarah am going to the store. ____________________
2. The birds sing in the trees. ____________________
3. Max and Emily is playing soccer. ____________________
4. Mom are cooking dinner in the kitchen. ____________________
5. We are eat lunch at school. ____________________
6. The dog sleeps on the couch. ____________________
7. Dad is reads a book in the living room. ____________________
8. The children is running in the park. ____________________
9. The cat are sleeping on the bed. ____________________
10. The students are study for their test. ____________________

Choose the correct word to complete the sentence.

11. Sarah and her brother (is | are) building a sandcastle at the beach.
12. The teacher (teaches | teaching) a lesson in the classroom.
13. The baby (is | are) crawling on the floor.
14. We (are | being) watching a movie at home.
15. The birds (fly | flying) high in the sky.

Present Simple vs Present Progressive Review

Read the paragraph below. Use the verbs in the box to correctly complete the story.

read	sleep	chase	go	sing
cook	play	watch	bloom	shine

In the morning, the sun (1) ____________ brightly in the sky, and the birds (2) ____________ sweetly in the trees. Sarah (3) ____________ her favorite book on the porch while her mom (4) ____________ breakfast. Max and Emily (5) ____________ with their toys, and the cat (6) ____________ on the couch. Dad (7) ____________ TV before he (8) ____________ to work. Outside, the flowers (9) ____________ in the garden, and the dog (10) ____________ its tail.

Choose the correct word to complete the sentence.

11. Sarah usually (reads/reading) a book before bedtime.
12. Right now, the kids (play/playing) in the backyard.
13. The flowers (bloom/blooming) beautifully in the garden every spring.
14. Max often (watches/watching) his favorite cartoons on Saturday mornings.
15. Look! The cat (sleeps/sleeping) peacefully on the windowsill.

Past Tense

Past tense verbs tell about an action that has already happened. These verbs end with “ed”.

Regular Past Tense Verbs (talk)							
Singular						Plural	
Positive	I talked.	You talked.	He talked.	She talked.	It talked.	We talked.	They talked.
Negative	I didn’t talk.	You didn’t talk.	He didn’t talk.	She didn’t talk.	It didn’t talk.	We didn’t talk.	They didn’t talk.
Question	Did you talk?	Did you talk?	Did he talk?	Did she talk?	Did it talk?	Did we talk?	Did they talk?

If the verb ends with an “e”, add a “d” to the end to make the verb past tense.

Regular Past Tense Verbs (bake)							
Singular						Plural	
Positive	I baked.	You baked.	He baked.	She baked.	It baked.	We baked.	They baked.
Negative	I didn’t bake.	You didn’t bake.	He didn’t bake.	She didn’t bake.	It didn’t bake.	We didn’t bake.	They didn’t bake.
Question	Did you bake?	Did you bake?	Did he bake?	Did she bake?	Did it bake?	Did we bake?	Did they bake?

If the verb ends with **a consonant + a vowel + a consonant**

Regular Past Tense Verbs (jog)							
	Singular					Plural	
Positive	I jogged.	You jogged.	He jogged.	She jogged.	It jogged.	We jogged.	They jogged.
Negative	I didn't jog.	You didn't jog.	He didn't jog.	She didn't jog.	It didn't jog.	We didn't jog.	They didn't jog.
Question	Did you jog?	Did you jog?	Did he jog?	Did she jog?	Did it jog?	Did we jog?	Did they jog?

Finally, if the verb ends with **a consonant followed by a y**, the y changes to an "i" then add "ed"

Regular Past Tense Verbs (cry)							
	Singular					Plural	
Positive	I cried.	You cried.	He cried.	She cried.	It cried.	We cried.	They cried.
Negative	I didn't cry.	You didn't cry.	He didn't cry.	She didn't cry.	It didn't cry.	We didn't cry.	They didn't cry.
Question	Did you cry?	Did you cry?	Did he cry?	Did she cry?	Did it cry?	Did we cry?	Did they cry?

Practice: Read the passage below. Circle all of the past tense verbs.

Yesterday, I visited the zoo. I wanted to see all the different animals. I looked at a penguin with an orange beak. I asked the zookeeper where they sleep. I learned that they stayed on the ice to sleep. I enjoyed spending the day watching as the penguins marched around their habitat. Later, I imitated them and walked home.

Practice: Choose the correct word from the box to complete the sentence by writing the verb correctly.

visit	run	chase	read	sing
cook	play	watch	shine	paint

1. Yesterday, Sarah ____________ soccer with her friends.
2. Max and Emily ____________ their grandparents last weekend.
3. The cat ____________ a mouse around the house.
4. Dad ____________ dinner for the family yesterday.
5. We ____________ a movie at the cinema last night.
6. The birds ____________ beautifully in the trees this morning.
7. Mom ____________ a bedtime story to us last night.
8. The dog ____________ around the park with its owner.
9. Sarah ____________ a picture in art class yesterday.
10. The sun ____________ brightly during our picnic yesterday.

Past irregular verbs

There are some verbs that will change their spelling when put into the past tense. There are over 100 irregular verbs like this; here are some of them.

Simple	Past	Simple	Past	Simple	Past
eat	ate	run	ran	sing	sang
take	took	buy	bought	catch	caught
make	made	sell	sold	Read	read
have	had	give	gave	write	wrote
go	went	see	saw	teach	taught

Practice Past Irregular Verbs: Write the verbs correctly to complete the journal entry.

Dear Diary,

Today was an exciting day! In the morning, I (1) ________ (wake) up early because I (2) ________ (have) a big test at school. After breakfast, I (3) ________ (run) to catch the bus, but I (4) ________ (miss) it! So, I (5) ________ (walk) to school instead. During the test, I (6) ________ (write) down all the answers carefully. Afterward, my friends and I (7) ________ (go) to the park for a picnic lunch. We (8) ________ (eat) sandwiches and played games until it started to rain. When I (9) ________ (arrive) home, I (10) ________ (do) my homework and then (11) ________ (have) dinner with my family.

I'm tired now, but it was a great day overall!
Love, Diana

Write about what you did this weekend. Try to have at least 7-10 sentences.

Present Simple Vs Past Simple Review:

Choose the correct tense to complete the sentence.

1. Sarah (play/plays/is playing) soccer every Saturday morning.

2. Right now, the kids (play/are playing/played) in the garden.

3. Max (visited/visits/is visiting) his grandparents last weekend.

4. Mom (cook/cooks/is cooking) dinner for the family right now.

5. We usually (watch/watches/are watching) a movie at home on Fridays.

6. The birds (sing/sings/are singing) beautifully in the trees every morning.

7. Dad (read/reads/is reading) a book in the living room last night.

8. The dog (run/runs/is running) around the park with its owner.

9. Sarah (paint/paints/is painting) a picture in art class yesterday.

10. The sun (shine/shines/is shining) brightly during our picnic yesterday.

11. Sarah and her brother (play/plays/are playing) in the yard right now.

12. Last summer, we (visit/visited/are visiting) the beach with our friends.

Future Tense

Future Tense verbs tell about what will happen in the future.
With these verbs, use **will + verb**.

Future Tense Verb (work)							
Singular						Plural	
Positive	I will write.	You will write.	He will write.	She will write.	It will write.	We will write.	They will write.
Negative	I didn't write.	You didn't write.	He didn't write.	She didn't write.	It didn't write.	We didn't write.	They didn't write.
Question	Did you write?	Did you write?	Did he write?	Did she write?	Did it write?	Did we write?	Did they write?

Practice: Future Tense
Find the future tense verbs in the story and circle them.

My name is Jessica,
and when I grow up, I want to be a doctor.
As a doctor, I will help sick people feel better. I will check their heartbeats, take their temperature, and give them medicine to help them get well. I will need to study hard in school to learn about the human body and how to treat different illnesses.
I will also need to go to medical school after I finish high school.
In medical school, I will learn even more about being a doctor.
I will work in a hospital or a clinic, and I will wear a white coat and a stethoscope around my neck. I can't wait to become a doctor and help people every day!

Write about what you want to be when you grow up. Make sure that you explain what you will do and what you will need to do to learn or do to prepare for this job. Try to have at least 7-10 sentences.

Verb Tense Review:

1. What is the correct present simple form of the verb "to be" in the sentence: "I _____ happy today"?

a) am
b) is
c) are
d) been

2. In the sentence "She _____ her homework every day after school, " which verb tense is used?

a) past simple
b) present continuous
c) present simple
d) future perfect

3. Choose the correct past simple form of the verb "to go" in the sentence: "Yesterday, we _____ to the park."

a) goes
b) go
c) going
d) went

4. What is the correct present continuous form of the verb "to play" in the sentence: "They _____ soccer in the park right now"?

a) play
b) playing
c) plays
d) played

5. Which sentence uses the future tense verb "will" correctly?

a) "I am will going to the party tomorrow."
b) "He will watches a movie tonight."
c) "They will be playing basketball after school."
d) "We will goes to the zoo yesterday."

6. In the sentence "The cat _____ on the couch," which verb tense is used?

a) present continuous
b) present perfect
c) past simple
d) present simple

7. Choose the correct past simple form of the verb "to eat" in the sentence: "Yesterday, she _____ pizza for dinner."

a) eats
b) eat
c) eaten
d) ate

8. What is the correct present simple form of the verb "to read" in the sentence: "He _____ books every night"?

a) read
b) reads
c) reading
d) readed

9. Which sentence uses the present continuous tense correctly?

a) "She will cooks dinner tonight."
b) "They is playing outside."
c) "We are watching a movie right now."
d) "He going to the store tomorrow."

10. In the sentence "Mom _____ dinner for us," which verb tense is used?

a) past simple
b) present simple
c) present continuous
d) past continuous

11. Choose the correct past simple form of the verb "to swim" in the sentence: "Last summer, we _____ in the ocean."

a) swim
b) swam
c) swimming
d) swims

12. What is the correct present continuous form of the verb "to write" in the sentence: "I _____ a letter to my friend"?

a) write
b) wrote
c) writing
d) written

13. Which sentence uses the past simple tense correctly?

a) "He play soccer every day."
b) "We are played with our toys."
c) "She danced at the party last night."
d) "They will sings at the concert tomorrow."

14. In the sentence "The flowers _____ in the garden," which verb tense is used?

a) present simple
b) present continuous
c) past simple
d) past continuous

15. Choose the correct present simple form of the verb "to run" in the sentence: "She _____ every morning."

a) run
b) running
c) runs
d) ran

16. What is the correct past simple form of the verb "to drink" in the sentence: "Yesterday, he _____ juice"?

a) drink
b) drank
c) drinking
d) drinks

17. Which sentence uses the present simple tense correctly?

a) "They are sings in the choir."
b) "She will dances at the recital."
c) "He reads books every day."
d) "We were going to the zoo tomorrow."

18. In the sentence "I _____ my homework," which verb tense is used?

a) present simple
b) past simple
c) present continuous
d) past continuous

19. Choose the correct past simple form of the verb "to sleep" in the sentence: "Last night, they _____ early."

a) sleep
b) sleeping
c) slept
d) sleeps

20. What is the correct present continuous form of the verb "to study" in the sentence: "She _____ for her test"?

a) studied
b) studying
c) studies
d) study

21. Which sentence uses the past simple tense correctly?

a) "He will writes a story yesterday."
b) "They were read a book last night."
c) "She danced at the party last night."
d) "We will going to the zoo tomorrow."

22. In the sentence "The dog _____ in the yard," which verb tense is used?

a) present simple
b) present continuous
c) past simple
d) past continuous

23. Choose the correct past simple form of the verb "to speak" in the sentence: "Last week, she _____ to her friend."

a) speak
b) speaking
c) spoke
d) speaks

24. What is the correct present simple form of the verb "to watch" in the sentence: "They _____ TV every evening"?

a) watch
b) watching
c) watched
d) watches

Modal verbs

Modal verbs are helping verbs that express certain conditions. They can be divided into three groups, verbs that describe ability, suggestion, and permission.

Ability: Can		
	Present Simple	Past Simple
Positive	Subject + can + verb. **I can sew** my own clothes.	Subject + could + verb. **Jon could swim** in the ocean
Negative	Subject + can't + verb. **Max can't ride** a bike.	Subject + couldn't + verb. **He couldn't find** his toy.
Question	Can + subject + verb. **Can you dance** the tango?	Could + subject + verb. **Could you read** at 3.

Ability: May		
	Present Simple	Past Simple
Positive	Subject + may + verb. If you are a good swimmer, **you may dive** off the boat.	
Negative	Subject + may not + verb. **You may not have** dessertbefore dinner.	
Question	May + subject + verb. **May I use** your crayons?	

Possibility/Permission: May, Might		
	Present Simple	Past Simple
Positive	Subject + may + verb. You may play outside after studying. I might come to the party late.	
Negative	Subject + may not + verb. You may not have any more cookies. He might not make it tonight.	
Question	May + subject + verb. May I borrow a pencil.	

Necessity: Must, need		
	Present Simple	Past Simple
Positive	Subject + must + verb. She must study for the test. You need to study for the test.	Subject + needed to + verb. She needed 3 points to get an A.
Negative	Subject + doesn't need + verb. You don't need to bring books.	Subject didn't need + verb. He didn't need to do that.
Question	Do/Does + subject + need to+ verb. Do you need to go?	Did + subject + need + verb. Did you need to take medicine?

Advice/Suggestion: Should		
	Present Simple	Past Simple
Positive	Subject + should + verb. You should drink more water.	Subject + should have + verb I should have brought a jacket.
Negative	Subject + shouldn't + verb. Children shouldn't talk to strangers.	Subject + shouldn't have + verb I shouldn't have eaten that.
Question	Should + subject + verb. Should I color my hair?	Should + subject + have + verb Should I have called first?

Modal Verb Practice

Fill in the blank with the correct modal verb. Some sentences could have multiple answers.

1. You ____________ eat vegetables to stay healthy.
2. We ____________ go to the park if it's sunny.
3. Sarah ____________ help her friend with homework.
4. I ____________ drink milk to make my bones strong.
5. Max ____________ clean his room before he plays.
6. You ____________ ask for help if you don't understand.
7. The teacher ____________ read a story to the class.
8. Mom ____________ bake cookies for us this weekend.
9. The cat ____________ sleep in its bed at night.
10. We ____________ say "please" and "thank you" to be polite.
11. You ____________ wear a helmet when riding a bike.
12. Sarah ____________ play with her toys after finishing her homework.
13. We ____________ listen to our parents to stay safe.
14. The birds ____________ sing sweetly in the morning.
15. I ____________ help my friend when they are sad.

Perfect Tense

Perfect tense verbs put an action in the context of another action. Perfect tense is still used in present, past, and future situations.

The **present perfect tense** tells about something that has happened or has started already that is related to something that is happening now. In these cases, the helping verb is used in its present tense form.

Everything **had looked** so much bigger when I was a kid, now it looks small

Present Perfect Tense (wash)							
Subject + has/have + past participle + predicate.							
	Singular					Plural	
Positive	I have washed my hands already.	You have washed your hands already.	He has washed his hands already.	She has washed her hands already.	It has washed its hands already.	We have washed our hands already.	They have washed their hands already.
Negative	I haven't washed my hands yet..	You haven't washed your hands yet..	He hasn't washed his hands yet..	She hasn't washed her hands yet..	It hasn't washed its hands yet..	We haven't washed our hands yet..	They haven't washed their hands yet..
Question	Have I washed my hands already?	Have you washed your hands already?	Has he washed his hands already?	Has she washed her hands already?	Has it washed its hands already?	Have we washed our hands already?	Have they washed their hands already?

Present-Perfect Practice: Complete the sentence.

1. Sarah ____________________ (finish) her homework.

2. We ____________________ (visit) the zoo.

3. Max ____________________ (clean) his room.

4. The cat ____________________ (eat) its food.

5. Mom ____________________ (cook) dinner for us.

6. They ____________________ (play) soccer.

7. I ____________________ (read) a book.

8. You ____________________ (do) your chores.

9. He ____________________ (build) a sandcastle.

10. She ____________________ (paint) a picture.

11. We ____________________ (not, forget) to feed the fish.

12. They ____________________ (not, see) the movie yet.

13. Has Sarah ____________________ (finish) her project?

14. Have you ____________________ (clean) your room yet?

Past Perfect Tense verbs tell about actions that have been completed and how it relates to another action that has also already been completed

I wanted to see Wonka, but my friend **had seen it** already.

Past Perfect Tense (leave)							
Subject + had + past participle + predicate.							
	Singular					Plural	
Positive	I had left.	You had left.	He had left.	She had left.	It had left.	We had left.	They had left.
Negative	I hadn't left for the day.	You hadn't left for the day.	He hadn't left for the day.	She hadn't left for the day.	It hadn't left for the day.	We hadn't left for the day.	They hadn't left for the day.
Question	Had I left for the day?	Had you left for the day?	Had he left for the day?	Had she left for the day?	Had it left for the day?	Had we left for the day?	Had they left for the day?

Past Perfect Practice: Correct the sentences below or write "correct" if there are no corrections to make.

1. Sarah had went to bed early last night. ____________________
2. Max had did his homework before dinner. ____________________
3. Mom had cook dinner when we arrived. ____________________
4. They had saw a movie after school. ____________________
5. I had finished my project before the deadline. ____________________
6. You had not did your chores yet. ____________________
7. He had went to the store yesterday. ____________________
8. We had visited our grandparents last weekend. ____________________
9. She had not went to the park with her friends. ____________________

Future Perfect Tense is used to tell about a future action that will take place and how it relates to a separate action also in the future.

Perfect tense typically puts a past event into the context of another event.

I **will have eaten** dinner by the time you get home.

Future Perfect Tense (finish)							
Subject + will have + past participle + predicate.							
Singular						Plural	
Positive	I will have finished my work by then.	You will have finished your work by then.	He will have finished his work by then.	She will have finished her work by then.	It will have finished its work by then.	We will have finished our work by then.	They will have finished their work by then.
Negative	I won't have finished my work by then.	You won't have finished your work by then.	He won't have finished his work by then.	She won't have finished her work by then.	It won't have finished its work by then.	We won't have finished our work by then.	They won't have finished their work by then.
Question	Will I have finished my work by then?	Will you have finished your work by then?	Will he have finished his work by then?	Will she have finished her work by then?	Will it have finished its work by then?	Will we have finished our work by then?	Will they have finished their work by then?

***Future Perfect Tense Practice**

By the time I finish school next year, I ________________ (complete) my project.

My family and I ____________________ (move) to a new house by then.

We ____________________ (live) in our current home for ten years.

My parents _________________________ (buy) the new house last month. By the time we move, we _________________________ (pack) all our belongings.

Perfect Tense Review:

1. Which sentence uses the future perfect tense?

    a) "Yesterday, I finished my homework."
    b) "By next summer, I will have planted flowers in the garden."
    c) "She is reading a book right now."
    d) "We visited the zoo last weekend."

2. What is the past perfect tense of the verb "to eat" in the sentence: "Yesterday, she ________ dinner"?

    a) eats
    b) eating
    c) ate
    d) eaten

3. Choose the correct past perfect tense of the verb "to play" in the sentence: "Before dinner, they ________ outside"?

    a) play
    b) played
    c) playing
    d) plays

4. Which sentence uses the present perfect tense correctly?

    a) "He will finish his homework yesterday."
    b) "They have went to the park last Saturday."
    c) "She has read three books this month."
    d) "We did the experiment yesterday."

5. What is the past perfect tense of the verb "to swim" in the sentence: "Yesterday, we ________ in the pool"?

    a) swim
    b) swam
    c) swimming
    d) swims

6. Choose the correct past perfect tense of the verb "to write" in the sentence: "Before the test, she ________ notes"?

    a) write
    b) wrote
    c) writing
    d) writes

7. Which sentence uses the present perfect tense correctly?

    a) "They have watched a movie last night."
    b) "He has go to the store today."
    c) "She has finished her homework already."
    d) "We will visit the museum tomorrow."

8. What is the future perfect tense of the verb "to study" in the sentence: "By next week, they ________ for the test"?

    a) study
    b) studied
    c) studying
    d) will have studied

9. Choose the correct past perfect tense of the verb "to sing" in the sentence: "Before the concert, they ________ songs"?

a) sing
b) sang
c) singing
d) sings

10. Which sentence uses the future perfect tense?

a) "She has danced at the party last night."
b) "They had played soccer yesterday."
c) "By next month, we will have finished the project."
d) "He swims in the pool every morning."

11. What is the past perfect tense of the verb "to drink" in the sentence: "Yesterday, he ________ juice"?

a) drink
b) drank
c) drinking
d) drinks

12. Choose the correct past perfect tense of the verb "to sleep" in the sentence: "Before the movie, she ________ for eight hours"?

a) sleep
b) slept
c) sleeping
d) sleeps

13. Which sentence uses the present perfect tense correctly?

a) "They have swim in the ocean yesterday."
b) "He have finished his homework."
c) "She has painted three pictures this week."
d) "We will play games at the party yesterday."

14. What is the future perfect tense of the verb "to run" in the sentence: "By next month, she ________ a marathon"?

a) run
b) ran
c) running
d) will have run

15. Choose the correct past perfect tense of the verb "to speak" in the sentence: "Before the presentation, they ________ about the topic"?

a) speak
b) spoke
c) speaking
d) speaks

16. Which sentence uses the present perfect tense correctly?

a) "He has went to the store."
b) "They have visited the museum tomorrow."
c) "She has read a book last night."
d) "We have finished our homework."

17. What is the future perfect tense of the verb "to write" in the sentence: "By the end of the month, she ________ her novel"?

a) write
b) wrote
c) writing
d) will have written

18. Choose the correct past perfect tense of the verb "to swim" in the sentence: "Before the race, he ________ across the lake"?

a) swim
b) swam
c) swimming
d) swims

19. Which sentence uses the present perfect tense correctly?

a) "They have read a book yesterday."
b) "He have gone to the zoo."
c) "She has finished her painting."
d) "We will go to the park tomorrow."

20. What is the future perfect tense of the verb "to dance" in the sentence: "By the end of the year, they ________ at the recital"?

a) dance
b) danced
c) dancing
d) will have danced

21. Choose the correct past perfect tense of the verb "to sleep" in the sentence: "Before the trip, they ________ for ten hours"?

a) sleep
b) slept
c) sleeping
d) sleeps

22. Which sentence uses the present perfect tense correctly?

a) "He has goes to the store."
b) "They have go to the beach."
c) "She has cooked dinner already."
d) "We will play soccer tomorrow."

23. What is the future perfect tense of the verb "to study" in the sentence: "By next month, he ________ for the exam"?

a) study
b) studied
c) studying
d) will have studied

24. Choose the correct past perfect tense of the verb "to eat" in the sentence: "Before the party, she ________ dinner"?

a) eat
b) ate
c) eating
d) eats

Subject-verb agreement

You have just gone over all the different types of verbs. Always remember to match the number of nouns in your subject to the correct verb. Singular subjects including the pronouns he, she, and it have an s, es, or ies at the end of the verb (depending on their spelling.) Plural subjects, including the pronouns we and they do not have an s at the end of the verb. Finally, I and you do not have an s at the end.

Regular Present Simple Verbs (walk)						
Singular					Plural	
I walk.	You walk.	He walks.	She walks.	It walks.	We walk.	They walk.

Subject verb agreement practice

Read the paragraph and find the six mistakes in subject verb agreement. Correct them in the paragraph.

A group of friendly animals live in the forest. Every morning, they wake up and goes for a walk together. The rabbit hops ahead, while the squirrel scurry beside. The birds sing happily as they fly overhead. Suddenly, they hears a loud noise. They stops and listens carefully. It sounds like thunder. The animals gets scared and run back to their homes. When the storm pass, they comes out again to play. They knows that as long as they stick together, they can face anything.

Read the story below and underline all the verbs you find.

Once upon a time, there was a curious cat named Whiskers. Every day, Whiskers would explore the neighborhood, chase butterflies, and climb trees. One day, Whiskers discovered a hidden path in the woods. Excitedly, Whiskers followed the path and found a magical garden at the end.

Fill in the blank with the given verb in the correct tense.

1. Sarah __________ (play) with her toys in the room now.
2. We __________ (finish) our project next week.
3. The birds __________ (sing) sweetly in the morning.
4. Yesterday, Max __________ (ride) his bike in the park.
5. By the time we arrive, they __________ (prepare) dinner.

Read the sentence below, if there is a mistake circle it and write the correction on the line. If there is no mistake write "Correct"

1. She is dance in the living room. ____________________
2. They has went to the beach last summer. ____________________
3. He will reads a book tomorrow. ____________________
4. Yesterday, we have went to the zoo. ____________________
5. By next month, they have finished the puzzle. ____________________

Use the words from the word bank to complete the sentence correctly

must could may might should

1. You ________ eat vegetables to stay healthy.
2. Sarah ________ help her friend with homework yesterday.
3. We ________ say "please" and "thank you" to be polite.
4. __________ I have a glass of water?
5. Next summer, my family ________ travel to Europe.

Fill in the blanks with the correct be verb.

1. She __________ going to the store.
2. They __________ happy with their new toys.
3. The cat __________ sleeping on the couch.
4. We __________ going to the park tomorrow.
5. He __________ my best friend.

Verb Test:

1. Choose the correct form of the "be verb" for the subject "I":

a) am
b) is
c) are

2. Which sentence uses the correct "be verb" for the subject "they"?

a) They is playing in the park.
b) They am playing in the park.
c) They are playing in the park.

3. Fill in the blank with the correct "be verb": She ________ a teacher.

a) am
b) is
c) are

4. What is the present tense of the verb "to play" in the sentence: "She ________ with her toys"?

a) plays
b) play
c) played

5. Which sentence uses the present tense correctly?

a) They plays in the garden.
b) He play soccer every day.
c) We play games at the party.

6. Fill in the blank with the correct present tense verb: The bird ________ in the tree.

a) fly
b) flies
c) flew

7. What is the present progressive tense of the verb "to run" in the sentence: "He ________ in the race"?

a) runs
b) run
c) running

8. Choose the correct present progressive tense verb: They ________ in the park.

a) play
b) played
c) are playing

9. Fill in the blank with the correct present progressive tense verb: The cat ________ on the bed.

a) sleeps
b) sleeping
c) is sleeping

10. What is the past tense of the verb "to jump" in the sentence: "She ________ over the fence"?

a) jumps
b) jump
c) jumped

11. Which sentence uses the past tense correctly?

a) They is playing outside yesterday.
b) He play with his friends last week.
c) We played soccer at the park.

12. Fill in the blank with the correct past tense verb: Sarah ________ to the store yesterday.

a) go
b) goes
c) went

13. What is the past perfect tense of the verb "to eat" in the sentence: "Yesterday, they ________ lunch"?

a) eat
b) ate
c) eating

14. Choose the correct past perfect tense verb: We ________ our homework before dinner.

a) do
b) did
c) doing

15. Fill in the blank with the correct past perfect tense verb: The dog ________ his bone before he went to sleep.

a) chew
b) chewed
c) chewing

16. What is the future tense of the verb "to read" in the sentence: "Tomorrow, she ________ a book"?

a) read
b) reads
c) reading

17. Choose the correct future tense verb: We ________ to the zoo next weekend.

a) go
b) goes
c) will go

18. Fill in the blank with the correct future tense verb: They ________ a movie tomorrow.

a) watch
b) watching
c) will watch

19. What is the future perfect tense of the verb "to finish" in the sentence: "By next month, they ________ the puzzle"?

a) finish
b) finishing
c) will have finished

20. Choose the correct future perfect tense verb: She ________ her homework by the end of the week.

a) will finish
b) finishing
c) finish

21. Fill in the blank with the correct future perfect tense verb: They ________ the race by the time we arrive.

a) finish
b) will finish
c) finishing

22. Which sentence uses the modal verb "should" correctly?

a) He can go to bed early tonight.
b) She will eat her vegetables for dinner.
c) You should brush your teeth before bed.

23. Choose the correct modal verb: We ________ wear a helmet when riding a bike.

a) can
b) should
c) might

24. Fill in the blank with the correct modal verb: They ________ study for the test tomorrow.

a) can
b) could
c) should

25. Which sentence uses the modal verb "can" correctly?

a) You would go to the park tomorrow.
b) She might read a book tonight.
c) They can swim in the pool.

26. Choose the correct modal verb: He ________ play soccer after school.

a) can
b) will
c) must

27. Fill in the blank with the correct modal verb: We ________ visit our grandparents next weekend.

a) can
b) could
c) will

28. Which sentence uses the correct verb tense?

a) She will eats dinner after homework.
b) They is going to the park tomorrow.
c) We have played games at the party.

케이스별 학생 컨설팅 전략

일반 초등학교 출신의 G4남학생

(Reading/ Writing : Fluent speaking/Listening: intermediate)

- 어라운즈와 함께 준비한 기간: 1개월

이 학생의 경우 리딩과 라이팅의 실력이 좋고 기본기가 탄탄했기 때문에 인터뷰 준비에 더욱 집중하는 등 실력이 좋아 시간적으로 여유가 있는 학생이었습니다.

강점이 있고, 기본기 또한 탄탄하여 쉬운 케이스였습니다.

- 어라운즈의 솔루션

단어를 많이 알고있었으며 기본기가 좋았기 때문에 바로 문제를 풀 수 있었습니다. 상대적으로 약한 스피킹에 시간을 많이 투자 했습니다. 적합한 단어 사용 그리고 문법 실수를 최소로 하기 위해 노력했습니다. 맵테스트는 250점을 받았고, 어라운즈와 인터뷰 준비를 하며 SJA에 합격하였습니다

Adjectives and adverbs

Prepositions

Linking Words

Commas

Abbreviation

Letter Writing

Adjectives

Remember that nouns are people, places, animals, ideas and things. You can describe or tell how that noun looks, sounds, tastes or smells using adjectives.

Example: It's a beautiful day.

Adjective Practice: Circle the noun in the sentence and then write the adjective that describes it in the box.

1. She has a black cat. ______________________
2. He is wearing a blue shirt. ______________________
3. The chicken is too spicy. ______________________
4. The loud bell rang at 9 am. ______________________
5. I like chocolate cake. ______________________
6. We smelled the sweet flowers. ______________________
7. They are sitting under a shady tree. ______________________
8. It's very hot today. ______________________
9. Look at the red balloon. ______________________
10. I am smart. ______________________

Use adjectives to describe the pictures in complete sentences.

Comparative & Superlative Adjectives

If you have two nouns and you want to compare them you can use comparative adjectives. This takes the regular adjective and adds "-er" to the end of it. Ex. tall**er**, short**er**, old**er**, happ**ier**, hott**er**.

If there are three or more nouns being compared, then you would use a superlative adjective. This takes the same adjective but adds "-est" to the end of it to show. Ex. tallest, shortest, oldest, happiest, hottest.

Practice: Circle the person that is being described.

Brian is the short boy with the blue shirt.

Brian's brother Dennis is **taller** than Brian.

Brian's dad is the **tallest** in the family.

Practice: Use the word provided to correctly complete the sentence.

1. sweet	Cherries are __________ than raspberries.
2. cold	This is the __________ winter ever!
3. short	I am ____________ than my brother.
4. tall	Mount Everest is the __________ mountain in the world.
5. old	My grandfather is ___________ than my grandmother.

Write a comparative paragraph about you and your family or your friends using comparative and superlative adjectives. Try to write 7-10 sentences.

Adverb

While adjectives describe nouns, adverbs describe verbs. An adverb tells you how, when, or where something is happening.

Adverbs that tell how something is happening are typically adjectives with "-ly" added to the end of it.

sweet	sweetly	happy	happily
loud	loudly	bright	brightly
quick	quickly	painful	painfully

Both words have similar meanings, but are attached to a different word.

The **stars** are <u>bright</u> tonight. | The stars **shine** <u>brightly</u> tonight.

Adverb Practice: Read the paragraph. Draw a square around the verbs and circle the adverbs. Draw a line to connect the verb and the adverb that describes it.

Once upon a time, there lived a young girl named Sarah. She lived happily in a cozy cottage at the edge of the forest. Every morning, Sarah woke up early and eagerly to explore the woods. She wandered deep into the forest, marveling at the towering trees and chirping birds. Sarah walked carefully along the winding paths, listening intently to the rustling leaves. Suddenly, she spotted a colorful butterfly fluttering gracefully among the flowers. Excitedly, Sarah chased after the butterfly, laughing joyously as it danced away.

Adverb & Adjective Practice: Use the word correctly to complete the sentence.

1. [lazy] The ________________ cat stretched lazily on the windowsill.

2. [brisk] She walked ________________ through the crowded market.

3. [beautiful] The __________ flowers bloomed beautifully in the garden.

4. [confident] He spoke ________________ during the presentation.

5. [happy] The ________________ bird chirped happily in the tree.

6. [melodious] She sang __________ during the talent show.

7. [excited] The __________ dog wagged its tail excitedly.

8. [energetic] They played __________ in the park all afternoon.

9. [graceful] The __________ butterfly fluttered gracefully in the breeze.

10. [quick] He ran __________ to catch the bus.

11. [loud] She sang __________ during the concert.

12. [happy] The children played __________ in the park.

13. [careful] He drove __________ to avoid hitting the deer.

14. [fast] The train moved __________ through the countryside.

15. [quiet] They tiptoed __________ into the room.

Adverbs of time tell you when something is happening.

Common Adverbs of Time				
afterwards	in November	soon	today	now
immediately	on Friday	eventually	later	before

Practice: Use the words from the box above to complete the story below.

Once upon a time, there was a little girl named Lily who lived in a small town. One chilly morning __________, Lily woke up excitedly because it was her birthday __________. She couldn't wait to open her presents! Her parents told her she had to wait until __________ after breakfast. Lily ate her pancakes as fast as she could, and __________, she was tearing the wrapping paper off her gifts. She got a new bicycle, a dollhouse, and a big box of art supplies. __________, she was outside riding her bike with her friends. __________, Lily realized she had to finish her homework __________ going to bed. But __________, she forgot about her homework and fell asleep. __________, Lily's mom woke her up, reminding her about her homework. Lily finished it __________ and crawled into bed, tired but happy after a wonderful birthday.

Adverbs of place tell **where** something is happening.

Common Adverbs of Place				
anywhere	out	on	right	upstairs
outside	east	indoors	off	under

Circle the best word to complete the sentence.

1. He searched [under | above] the bed for his lost toy.
2. The cat jumped [up | down] from the tree branch.
3. They sat [inside | outside] the cafe, enjoying their coffee.
4. The ball rolled [across | around] the playground.
5. She placed her backpack [near | far] the door before leaving.
6. The birds flew [high | low] in the sky.
7. The squirrel hid [behind | in front of] the tree trunk.
8. The children played [beside | under] the school building.
9. The fish swam [around | under] the coral reef.
10. They walked [along | across] the sandy beach, collecting seashells.

Prepositions

Prepositions and adverbs of place/time are very similar to each other and are often even the same words. However they are different in how they relate to the words around them.

An adverb is strictly describing how, when, or where, a verb is happening and is typically seen behind the verb. Although it can also come before it.

He ran **quickly**.

She left on **Friday**.

We played **outside**.

Prepositions on the other hand, are describing a noun or the object of the sentence and will be in front of the object of the sentence.

He ran quickly **down** the path.

She left on Friday **before** breakfast.

We played outside **near** my house.

Common Prepositions				
above	behind	beside	between	by
next to	in front of	under	outside	in
around	below	up	into	with

Preposition Practice:

Use the picture to answer the questions.

1) Where is the cat?

The cat is sitting ________ the rug.

2) Where is the basket?

The basket is___________ the desk.

3) Where is the pink blanket?

The blanket is ______________ the mom's feet.

4) Where is the clock?

The clock is _________ the plant and the books.

5) Where is the lamp?

The lamp is _________ the chair.

6) Where is the red chair?

The chair is____________ the window.

More Conjunctions

There are many other conjunctions, often called transition words that can also be used to connect sentences. There are well over 50 conjunctions but these are the most popular.

If	Since	As	When	Although
I'll change my plans **if** it rains	You should get the dress **since** you like it.	You are in charge **as** you are the oldest.	I learned to drive **when** I was 18.	**Although** I like ketchup, I don't like tomatoes.
While	**After**	**Before**	**Until**	**Because**
I'll cut out the pieces **while** you glue them down.	She thanked everyone **after** accepting her award.	She took a deep breath **before** jumping in the water.	You can't go outside **until** you finish your homework.	She got sunburn **because** she didn't put on any sunblock.

Subordinating Conjunction Practice: Choose the best conjunction to complete the sentence.

1. Sarah couldn't sleep ________________ she drank a cup of warm milk.
2. Tom always wears his raincoat ________________ it's raining outside.
3. We played games at the park ________________ the sun was shining.
4. Mary always brushes her teeth ________________ she goes to bed.
5. The cat slept peacefully ______________ the children were playing loudly.
6. Max waited patiently ________________ his friends arrived at the party.
7. The flowers bloomed beautifully ________________ it had rained heavily the night before.
8. Alex didn't eat his vegetables ________________ he was hungry.
9. The birds chirped happily ________________ the sun rose in the sky.
10. Dad mowed the lawn ____________________ it started to rain.

Adjective & Adverb Review:

Circle the noun and underline the adjective that describes it.

1. The red apple fell from the tree.
2. She has a beautiful smile.
3. It was a rainy day yesterday.
4. The small puppy followed me home.
5. He wears a blue shirt every Monday.

Circle the verb and the adverb that describes it.

6. She speaks softly to avoid waking the baby.
7. He ran quickly to catch the bus.
8. The sun is shining brightly in the sky.
9. They played happily in the park all afternoon.
10. The dog barked loudly when the doorbell rang.

Circle the best word to complete the sentence.

11. Sarah is the (fast | faster | fastest) runner on the team.
12. This is the (big | bigger | biggest) cake I've ever seen!
13. The elephant is (large | larger | largest) than the mouse.
14. Today is (hot | hotter | hottest) than yesterday.
15. The red car is (expensive | more expensive | most expensive) than the blue one.

Circle the preposition in the sentence.

16. The book is on the table.
17. The cat jumped over the fence.
18. She walked to the store.
19. The keys are under the mat.
20. He sat beside his friend.

Circle the best word to complete the sentence.

21. She arrived at the party (earlier | late) than expected.
22. The children played (outside | inside) until it started raining.
23. They went for a walk (yesterday | tomorrow) afternoon.
24. The store opens (soon | later) in the day.
25. The cat sleeps (under | above) the bed every night.
26. He finished his homework (quickly | slower) than usual.
27. We will have dinner (here | up) tonight.
28. She went to the library (yesterday | today) to borrow some books.
29. They waited (patiently | impatiently) for the bus to arrive.
30. The concert begins (soon | far) after sunset.

Adjective & Adverb Test:

1. Identify the comparative form of the adjective: "The giraffe is tall, but the elephant is even ________."

   a) taller
   b) tall
   c) tallest

2. Choose the superlative form of the adjective: "Mount Everest is the ________ mountain in the world."

   a) tall
   b) tallest
   c) taller

3. Choose the correct adverb to complete the sentence: "She sings ________."

   a) loudly
   b) loud
   c) louder

4. Choose the correct adverb to complete the sentence: "He solved the puzzle ________ than his sister."

   a) quick
   b) quicker
   c) quickest

5. Identify the superlative form of the adjective: "This is the ________ book I've ever read."

   a) interesting
   b) more interesting
   c) most interesting

6. Choose the correct comparative form of the adjective: "She runs ________ than her brother."

   a) fast
   b) faster
   c) fastest

7. Choose the correct preposition to complete the sentence: "The cat is ________ the table."

   a) on
   b) in
   c) under

8. Choose the correct preposition to complete the sentence: "We walked ________ the park."

   a) to
   b) at
   c) over

9. Choose the correct adverb of time to complete the sentence: "She will arrive __________."

a) later
b) late
c) lately

10. Choose the correct adverb of place to complete the sentence: "The keys are __________ the drawer."

a) inside
b) outside
c) beside

11. Choose the correct adverb of time to complete the sentence: "We went to the beach __________."

a) yesterday
b) tomorrow
c) today

12. Identify the superlative form of the adjective: "This is the ________ movie I've ever seen."

a) good
b) better
c) best

13. Choose the correct comparative form of the adjective: "The elephant is ________ than the lion."

a) big
b) bigger
c) biggest

14. Choose the correct preposition to complete the sentence: "The cat is __________ the box."

a) over
b) under
c) beside

15. Choose the correct preposition to complete the sentence: "We walked __________ the bridge."

a) across
b) through
c) above

16. Choose the correct adverb of time to complete the sentence: "He finished his homework __________."

a) quick
b) quickly
c) quicker

Adjective & Adverb Test:

17. Choose the correct adverb of place to complete the sentence: "The birds are flying __________ the trees."

a) under
b) between
c) among

18. Identify the superlative form of the adjective: "This is the ________ cake I've ever tasted."

a) delicious
b) more delicious
c) most delicious

19. Choose the correct comparative form of the adjective:
"She is __________ than her sister."

a) smart
b) smarter
c) smartest

20. Choose the correct preposition to complete the sentence:
"The book is __________ the shelf."

a) below
b) on
c) above

21. Choose the correct preposition to complete the sentence:
"We sat __________ the table."

a) behind
b) on
c) below

22. Choose the correct adverb of time to complete the sentence:
"The train will arrive __________."

a) soon
b) sooner
c) soonest

23. Choose the correct adverb of place to complete the sentence:
"The ball rolled __________ the stairs."

a) up
b) down
c) across

24. Identify the superlative form of the adjective: "This is the ________ day of my life."

a) happy
b) happier
c) happiest

25. Choose the correct comparative form of the adjective:
"The mountain is __________ than the hill."

a) high
b) higher
c) highest

COMMAS

Commas are a very useful punctuation mark. When writing about multiple objects or actions, a comma can be used to separate the items in a list.

The four elements are fire, water, earth, and wind.
Brian enjoys playing basketball, reading comics, and painting.

List Comma Practice: Put the commas in the correct place.

1. I bought apples oranges bananas and grapes at the grocery store.
2. She packed her clothes shoes socks and toiletries for the trip.
3. We need to bring our pencils notebooks erasers and textbooks to class.
4. He enjoys playing soccer basketball baseball and tennis in his free time.
5. I visited Paris London Rome and Madrid during my European vacation.
6. My favorite colors are red blue yellow and green.
7. We need to buy bread milk eggs and butter from the store.
8. The menu includes pasta salad pizza and sandwiches for lunch.
9. She owns a cat dog rabbit and hamster as pets.
10. They watched movies played board games sang songs and danced at the party.

Commas are also used in dates. When writing the date, place a comma between the day and the year.

Jongkook was born September 1, 1997.
I moved to Korea on June 7, 2019.

Date Writing Practice: Write the date as Month Day, Year

1. What is today's date?

____

2. What was yesterday's date?

____

3. What is tomorrow's date?

____

4. When were you born?

____

5. When was your mom born?

____

6. When was your grandpa born?

____

7. When is Valentines Day?

____

8. When is White Day?

____

9. When is Pepero Day?

____

10. When is New Years Eve?

____

When you are writing about places, use a comma between the city and state or city and country.

My teacher is from Chicago, IL.

My mother was born in Busan, South Korea.

Location Comma Practice: Put the comma in the correct place in the sentence.

1. We visited Paris France last summer.
2. They went to the beach in Santa Monica California for vacation.
3. She lives in New York City New York.
4. The Eiffel Tower in Paris France is an iconic landmark.
5. Have you been to London England before?
6. My friend is from Tokyo Japan.
7. We traveled to Rome Italy for sightseeing.
8. They're going to visit Sydney Australia next month.
9. He moved to Los Angeles California for work.
10. The Great Wall of China in Beijing China is a must-see attraction.
11. She dreams of living in Venice Italy one day.
12. They're planning a trip to Cairo Egypt.
13. Have you ever been to Barcelona Spain?
14. My grandparents live in Toronto Canada.
15. We explored the Grand Canyon in Arizona USA during our road trip.

This paragraph is missing 8 commas. Put them in the correct places.

Last summer I went on a memorable vacation with my family. We visited France England and Italy during our trip. On July 15 2023 we explored the Eiffel Tower in Paris France and enjoyed breathtaking views of the city. Then, on July 20 2023, we took a scenic boat tour along the River Thames in London England. Finally, on July 25 2023, we marveled at the ancient ruins of the Colosseum in Rome Italy. It was an unforgettable experience that I will always cherish.

Circle the correct answer.

1. Which sentence is written correctly?

a) She enjoys reading, writing, and drawing in her free time.
b) She enjoys reading writing and drawing in her free time.
c) She enjoys reading writing and, drawing in her free time.

2. Choose the sentence that is written correctly.

a) The dog barked loudly, ran quickly, and jumped high.
b) The dog barked loudly ran quickly and jumped high.
c) The dog barked loudly, ran quickly and jumped high.

3. Which sentence is punctuated correctly?

a) They visited Paris, France, and London, England during their trip.
b) They visited Paris, France and London, England during their trip.
c) They visited Paris France, and London England during their trip.

4. **Select the sentence with correct punctuation.**
a) My favorite fruits are apples oranges and bananas.
b) My favorite fruits are apples, oranges, and bananas.
c) My favorite fruits are apples oranges, and bananas.

5. **Choose the sentence with the correct use of commas.**
a) He enjoys playing soccer basketball baseball and tennis.
b) He enjoys playing soccer basketball, baseball and tennis.
c) He enjoys playing soccer basketball baseball, and tennis.

6. **Which sentence is punctuated correctly?**
a) We need to buy bread, milk, eggs, and butter from the store.
b) We need to buy bread milk eggs and butter from the store.
c) We need to buy bread milk, eggs, and butter from the store.

7. **Select the sentence with correct punctuation.**
a) She lives in New York City, New York.
b) She lives in New York City New York.
c) She lives in New York City, New York.

8. **Choose the sentence with the correct use of commas.**
a) They're going to visit Sydney Australia next month.
b) They're going to visit Sydney, Australia, next month.
c) They're going to visit Sydney Australia, next month.

9. **Which sentence is written correctly?**
a) Have you been to Barcelona, Spain?
b) Have you been to Barcelona Spain?
c) Have you been to Barcelona, Spain.

10. **Choose the sentence that is punctuated correctly.**
a) The Great Wall of China, Beijing, is a must-see attraction.
b) The Great Wall of China Beijing is a must-see attraction.
c) The Great Wall of China, Beijing is a must-see attraction.

Read the sentence, if there is a mistake, circle it and write the correction on the line. If there are no mistakes, write "Correct".

1. She want to go to the store to buy some milk. ____________________

2. The cat sat on the mat, and licked its paws clean. ____________________

3. We're going too the beach for a picnic tomorrow. ____________________

4. They're going to Paris, London, and Rome. ____________________

5. He enjoys playing soccer, basketball, and tennis. ____________________

6. Have you been to Barcelona Spain? ____________________

7. The dog barked loudly, ran quickly, and jumped high. ____________________

8. She lives in New York City, New York. ____________________

9. My favorite fruits are apples oranges, and bananas. ____________________

10. The children played outside, until it started raining. ____________________

PunctuationTest:

1. Which sentence is punctuated correctly?

a) She enjoys playing soccer basketball baseball and tennis.

b) She enjoys playing soccer basketball, baseball and tennis.

c) She enjoys playing soccer, basketball, baseball, and tennis.

2. Select the sentence with correct punctuation.

a) My favorite colors are red blue yellow and green.

b) My favorite colors are red, blue, yellow, and green.

c) My favorite colors are red, blue yellow, and green.

3. Choose the sentence with the correct use of commas.

a) He likes to read books, watch movies, and play video games.

b) He likes to read books watch movies and play video games.

c) He likes to read books, watch movies and play video games.

4. Which sentence is written correctly?

a) The dog barked loudly ran quickly and jumped high.

b) The dog barked loudly, ran quickly, and jumped high.

c) The dog barked loudly, ran quickly and jumped high.

5. Select the sentence with correct punctuation.

a) They visited Paris France and London England during their trip.

b) They visited Paris, France, and London, England during their trip.

c) They visited Paris France, and London England during their trip.

6. Choose the sentence with the correct use of commas.

a) We need to buy bread milk eggs and butter from the store.

b) We need to buy bread, milk, eggs, and butter from the store.

c) We need to buy bread, milk eggs, and butter from the store.

7. Which sentence is punctuated correctly?

a) She lives in New York City New York.

b) She lives in New York City, New York.

c) She lives in New York City, New York,.

8. Select the sentence with correct punctuation.

a) The Great Wall of China, Beijing is a must-see attraction.
b) The Great Wall of China Beijing is a must-see attraction.
c) The Great Wall of China, Beijing, is a must-see attraction.

9. Choose the sentence with the correct use of commas.

a) They're going to visit Sydney Australia next month.
b) They're going to visit Sydney, Australia, next month.
c) They're going to visit Sydney Australia, next month.

10. Which sentence is written correctly?

a) Have you been to Barcelona, Spain?
b) Have you been to Barcelona Spain?
c) Have you been to Barcelona, Spain.

11. Which sentence is punctuated correctly?

a) The cat sat on the mat and licked its paws clean.
b) The cat sat on the mat, and licked its paws clean.
c) The cat sat on the mat, and, licked its paws clean.

12. Select the sentence with correct punctuation.

a) We visited Paris, France London, England and Rome, Italy.
b) We visited Paris, France, London, England, and Rome, Italy.
c) We visited Paris France London England and Rome Italy.

13. Choose the sentence with the correct use of commas.

a) I want to eat pizza spaghetti and salad for dinner.
b) I want to eat pizza, spaghetti, and salad for dinner.
c) I want to eat pizza, spaghetti and, salad for dinner.

14. Which sentence is written correctly?

a) They're going to the zoo tomorrow.
b) They're going too the zoo tomorrow.
c) They're going to the zoo, tomorrow.

17. **Which sentence is punctuated correctly?**
   a) My birthday is June 12 2008.
   b) My birthday is June, 12, 2008.
   c) My birthday is June 12, 2008.

18. **Select the sentence with correct punctuation.**
   a) We'll be at the park at 2:00 p.m.
   b) We'll be at the park at 2:00, p.m.
   c) We'll be at the park at 2:00 p.m..

19. **Choose the sentence with the correct use of commas.**
   a) She lives in Chicago Illinois.
   b) She lives in Chicago, Illinois.
   c) She lives in Chicago, Illinois,.

20. **Which sentence is written correctly?**
   a) Have you seen the movie Frozen 2?
   b) Have you seen the movie, Frozen, 2?
   c) Have you seen the movie, Frozen 2?

21. **Which sentence is punctuated correctly?**
   a) We're going to the beach, on Saturday, May 30th, 2024.
   b) We're going to the beach on Saturday May 30th, 2024.
   c) We're going to the beach on Saturday, May 30th, 2024.

22. **Select the sentence with correct punctuation.**
   a) She wants to buy a new dress, shoes, and a hat for the party.
   b) She wants to buy a new dress, shoes and, a hat for the party.
   c) She wants to buy a new dress shoes, and a hat for the party.

23. **Choose the sentence with the correct use of commas.**
   a) They traveled to Tokyo, Japan and, Seoul, South Korea during their vacation.
   b) They traveled to Tokyo, Japan, and Seoul, South Korea, during their vacation.
   c) They traveled to Tokyo Japan, and Seoul South Korea during their vacation.

24. Which sentence is written correctly?

a) My favorite subjects are Math, Science, and English.
b) My favorite subjects are Math Science and, English.
c) My favorite subjects are Math, Science, and English.

25. Select the sentence with correct punctuation.

a) We'll be arriving at the airport at 3:45 p.m., on Thursday, April 25th, 2024.
b) We'll be arriving at the airport at 3:45 p.m. on Thursday, April 25th, 2024.
c) We'll be arriving at the airport, at 3:45 p.m., on Thursday April 25th, 2024.

26. Choose the sentence with the correct use of commas.

a) She wants to eat pizza, spaghetti and salad for dinner.
b) She wants to eat pizza spaghetti and salad for dinner.
c) She wants to eat pizza spaghetti, and, salad for dinner.

27. Which sentence is punctuated correctly?

a) His birthday is December 10 2010.
b) His birthday is December, 10, 2010.
c) His birthday is December 10, 2010.

28. Select the sentence with correct punctuation.

a) They're planning to visit Washington D.C., and New York City during their trip.
b) They're planning to visit Washington D.C., and, New York City during their trip.
c) They're planning to visit Washington D.C. and New York City, during their trip.

29. Choose the sentence with the correct use of commas.

a) The picnic will be at the park, near the lake.
b) The picnic will be at the park near the lake.
c) The picnic will be, at the park, near the lake.

30. Which sentence is written correctly?

a) The movie starts at 7:00 p.m., on Friday, May 3rd.
b) The movie starts at 7:00 p.m. on Friday May 3rd.
c) The movie starts at 7:00 p.m. on Friday, May 3rd.

ABBREVIATIONS

Abbreviations are a short version of a longer word. Days and months are commonly abbreviated. To do this take the first three to four letters, followed by a period. Days of the week and months of the year are commonly abbreviated this way.

Abbreviated Day and Month Practice: Complete the chart.

Sunday	→	Sun.	April	→	
Monday	→	Mon.	May	→	X
Tuesday	→		June	→	X
	→	Wed.	July	→	X
Thursday	→			→	Aug.
	→	Fri.	September	→	
Saturday	→			→	Oct.
January	→	Jan.	November	→	
February	→			→	Dec.
	→	Mar.		→	

Another common abbreviation is for people's titles. They are shortened in various ways. Here are some common abbreviations for people's titles. It is important to note that title abbreviations should only be used when it is attached to a name but not in a regular sentence.

Good Example: Dr. Smith is a pediatrician at Mercy West Hospital.

Bad Example: My father is a Dr. at Mercy West Hospital.

Good Example: David Johnson Sr. is an architect.

Bad Example: I am a Sr. in high school.

First and last letter abbreviation

Doctor → Dr. Mister → Mr. Junior → Jr. Saint → St.

Miss → Ms. Senior → Sr.

First three to four letters

Captain → Capt. Professor → Prof. Senator → Sen. Reverend → Rev.

Representative → Rep. President → Pres.

Consonants

Private → Pvt. Sergeant → Sgt.

Abbreviated Title Practice: Rewrite the sentence with the correct abbreviation.

1. Doctor Johnson is our family physician.

____

2. Professor Smith teaches history at the university.

____

3. Captain Thompson leads the sailing expedition.

____

4. Reverend Davis delivered a powerful sermon last Sunday.

____

5. Lieutenant Roberts serves in the military.

____

6. Principal Garcia oversees the school's operations.

____

7. Sergeant Brown received a medal for bravery.

____

8. Attorney Patel specializes in immigration law.

____

9. Colonel Johnson retired after 30 years of service.

____

10. Detective Ramirez solved the case quickly.

____

Practice: Read the sentences. If there is a mistake, circle it and write the correction on the line. If there are no mistakes, write "correct".

1. Prof. Anderson teaches Biology. ________________
2. My uncle is a Lt. in the army. ________________
3. Mrs. Lopez is giving a presentation. ________________
4. Capt. Smith will be piloting the plane to New York. ________________
5. Dr. Brown is a renowned surgeon at the hospital. ________________

Units of measurement are often abbreviated in installation manuals, directions, and recipes. Here are some common abbreviations for American and International units of measure.

Measurements of Length & Distance

Inch → in. Feet → ft. Yards → yd. Miles → mi.
Centimeter→ cm. Kilometer → km. Meter → m

Measurements of Mass and Volume

Liter → L Milliliter → mL Gallon → gal. Cup → c.
Teaspoon →tsp. Tablespoon → tbsp. Quart → qt. Gram → g.
Kilogram → kg. Pound → lb. Ounce → oz.

Abbreviations for Units of Measurement Practice: Write the word for the abbreviation shown.

in. ________	yd ________	g. ________
m ________	mL ________	L ________
c. ________	tsp ________	oz ________
g. ________	qt. ________	tbsp ________
	kg. ________	lb. ________

Abbreviations are also helpful when writing addresses. Streets, states, and countries can all be abbreviated. Here are some examples of abbreviations.

Abbreviated Streets

Street → St. Place → Pl. Avenue → Ave. Lane → Ln.

Abbreviated State Names

Illinois → IL New Mexico → NM Arizona → AZ Maryland →MD
Deleware → DE Florida → FL Georgia → GA

Abbreviated Country Names

Germany → DEU Japan → JPN JAustralia → AUS JMexico → MEX
France → FRA JUnited States of America → USA JKorea → KOR

Abbreviated Address Practice: Rewrite the addresses with all the possible abbreviations.

BTS Jungkook ______________________

Loans Post Office Box #1062 ______________________

Donghwa Building Room. 201 ______________________

4 Wangsan-ro, Dongdaemun gu, ______________________

Seoul, South Korea ______________________

Dwayne "The Rock" Johnson ________________________________

224 Palermo Avenue ________________________________

COral Gables, Florida 33134 ________________________________

United States of America ________________________________

Bruce Wayne ________________________________

1007 Mountain Drive ________________________________

Gotham City, New Jersey 08701 ________________________________

United States of America ________________________________

Elena Neves ________________________________

4321 Los Dinos Circle ________________________________

Las Palmas, Canary Islands ________________________________

Spain ________________________________

Doctor Stephen Strange ________________________________

177A Bleecker Street ________________________________

New York City, New York 10012 ________________________________

United States of America ________________________________

Thor Odenson ________________________________

79 Tesseract Square ________________________________

Tonsberg, New Asgard 3110 ________________________________

Norway ________________________________

Abbreviations Review:

Directions: Write the correct abbreviation for each given term.

1. Doctor ____________________
2. Thursday ____________________
3. Kilometers ____________________
4. Mrs. ____________________
5. January ____________________
6. Professor ____________________
7. Inches ____________________
8. Monday ____________________
9. Boulevard ____________________
10. February ____________________
11. Street ____________________
12. Yards ____________________
13. Miss ____________________
14. March ____________________
15. Avenue ____________________
16. Wednesday ____________________
17. June ____________________
18. Road ____________________
19. September ____________________
20. Kilometers ____________________
21. December ____________________

Abbreviations Test:

Choose the correct abbreviation for each given term.

1. What is the abbreviation for the month of January?

a) Jan.
b) Jn.
c) Janu.

2. Which abbreviation stands for "Doctor"?

a) Dr.
b) Doc.
c) Doct.

3. What is the abbreviation for the day "Thursday"?

a) Thur.
b) Thurs.
c) Thu.

4. Which abbreviation represents "Inches"?

a) in.
b) inch.
c) inc.

5. What is the correct abbreviation for "Street"?

a) Str.
b) St.
c) Strt.

6. Which abbreviation stands for "February"?

a) Feb.
b) Febu.
c) Febra.

7. What is the abbreviation for "Professor"?

a) Pro.
b) Prof.
c) Profes.

8. What is the abbreviation for "Avenue"?

a) Ave.
b) Av.
c) Aven.

9. Which abbreviation represents "Miles"?

a) m.
b) mi.
c) mil.

10. What is the correct abbreviation for "Monday"?

a) Mond.
b) Mon.
c) Monda.

11. What is the abbreviation for "March"?

a) Mrch.
b) Mar.
c) Mch.

12. Which abbreviation stands for "Miss"?

a) Mis.
b) Ms.
c) Miss.

13. What is the abbreviation for "Road"?
a) Rd.
b) Ro.
c) R.

14. What is the abbreviation for "Kilometers"?
a) km.
b) kilo.
c) klm.

15. Which abbreviation represents "Thursday"?
a) Thur.
b) Thu.
c) Th.

16. What is the abbreviation for "June"?
a) Jun.
b) Juno.
c) Jne.

17. Which abbreviation stands for "Mrs."?
a) Mss.
b) Mrs.
c) Mrrs.

18. What is the abbreviation for "Yards"?
a) yd.
b) yrds.
c) yds.

19. Which abbreviation represents "Wednesday"?
a) Wedn.
b) Wed.
c) Wd.

20. What is the abbreviation for "Doctor"?
a) Doc.
b) Dr.
c) Doct.

21. What is the abbreviation for "Boulevard"?
a) Blvd.
b) Blvd
c) Bld.

22. Which abbreviation stands for "December"?
a) Decm.
b) Dec.
c) Dece.

23. What is the abbreviation for "Inches"?
a) inch.
b) in.
c) ich.

24. What is the abbreviation for "Thursday"?
a) Thurs.
b) Thur.
c) Thrs.

25. Which abbreviation represents "September"?
a) Sep.
b) Spt.
c) Sepr.

LETTER WRITING

Let's say that you are a huge fan of Michelle Yeoh and want to let her know. You can send her a letter or Fan Mail. Your letter should follow this format.

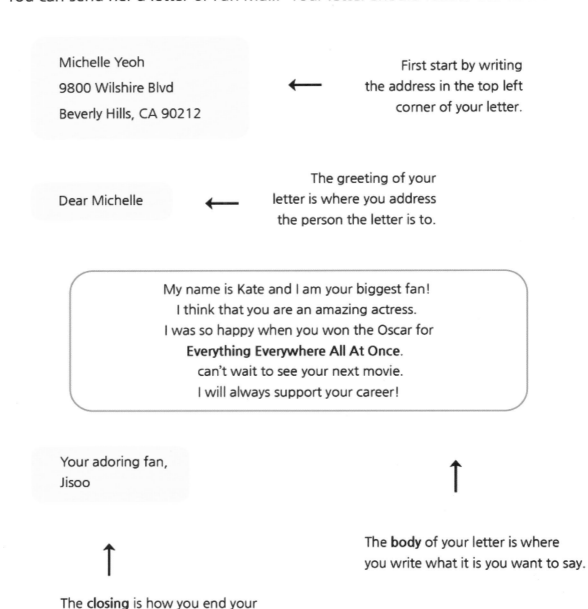

Michelle Yeoh
9800 Wilshire Blvd
Beverly Hills, CA 90212

← First start by writing the address in the top left corner of your letter.

Dear Michelle

← The greeting of your letter is where you address the person the letter is to.

My name is Kate and I am your biggest fan!
I think that you are an amazing actress.
I was so happy when you won the Oscar for
Everything Everywhere All At Once.
can't wait to see your next movie.
I will always support your career!

Your adoring fan,
Jisoo

↑ The **body** of your letter is where you write what it is you want to say.

↑ The **closing** is how you end your letter and sign your name.

Depending on who you are writing to, your letter format and writing style will be different. If you are writing to a professional organization, such as a school admissions office, or a company manager, or even your parents, you want to be more polite. On the other hand if you are just writing to a friend or your favorite celebrity it is okay to be less formal.

	Formal	Informal
Greeting	• Dear Mr. Obama, • To Whom It May Concern, • Dear Sir or Madam, • Dear Robbie Turner,	• Barack, • Hey Bestie! • Hello! • Good Morning!
	Your formal greeting should end with a comma but an informal greeting can use a comma or exclamation point. Formal greetings must never use only the first name of the recipient because you do not know them well.	
Body	• Introduce yourself and the reason for your letter. • Go into greater detail and explanation about the reason for your letter.	• No need to introduce yourself. • Detail why you are writing.
	A formal letter can be 1-3 paragraphs separating your introduction and details. There are no rules for the body of an informal letter.	
Closing	• Sincerely, • Regards, • Yours truly,	• TTYL • Laters! • Love
	Follow the rules of the greeting.	

Letter Writing Practice: Choose an address from the Address Abbreviation questions and write a formal letter to that person.

Letter Writing Practice: Think of your favorite book. Write an informal letter to your favorite character from that book.

Letter Writing Practice: Write a letter to your parents or a friend.

Letter Writing Test:

Answer the questions.

1. What is the correct way to write the date in a letter?

a) December 25, 2023
b) 25 December, 2023
c) 2023-12-25

2. Which of the following is the correct format for the recipient's address in a letter?

a) 123 Maple Street
Anytown, USA
Postal Code: 12345
b) Anytown, USA
123 Maple Street
Postal Code: 12345
c) Postal Code: 12345
123 Maple Street
Anytown, USA

3. In a formal letter, where should the sender's address be placed?

a) At the top left corner
b) At the bottom right corner
c) In the center of the page

4. What should be included in the salutation of a letter?

a) The sender's name
b) The recipient's name and title
c) The date

5. Which of the following is a suitable opening for a formal letter?

a) "Hey!"
b) "Dear Mr. Smith,"
c) "Hi there!"

6. What should be included in the body of a letter?

a) The closing
b) The sender's address
c) The main message or purpose of the letter

7. Which of the following is an appropriate way to end a formal letter?

a) "See you later!"
b) "Best regards,"
c) "Sincerely yours,"

8. What should you do before writing a letter to someone?

a) Nothing, just start writing.
b) Plan what you want to say.
c) Include jokes to make it interesting.

9. Which of the following is a polite way to ask for something in a letter?

a) "Give me this!"
b) "I want this!"
c) "Could you please send me..."

10. In a thank you letter, when should you express gratitude?

a) At the beginning
b) In the middle
c) At the end

11. Which of the following is an important aspect of writing a clear letter?

a) Using complicated words
b) Writing long, complex sentences
c) Keeping sentences short and simple

12. Identify the error in the following sentence: "Dear Ms. Johnson"

a) No error
b) The salutation is missing
c) "Ms." should be "Mrs."

13. Which of the following is the correct spelling?

a) Sincerely, yours truly
b) Sinserely, yours truly
c) Sincerly, yours truely

14. Identify the correct punctuation: "Thank you for your help"

a) Thank you for your help.
b) Thank you for your help,
c) Thank you for your help!

15. Choose the sentence that uses the correct capitalization:

a) "i will send you a letter soon."
b) "I will send you a letter soon."
c) "i Will send you a letter soon."

16. Write a suitable opening for a letter to your friend inviting them to your birthday party.

____

17. Imagine you're writing a letter to a pen pal in another country. What information about your country would you include in the letter?

____

18. Write a closing for a thank you letter to your teacher for helping you with a school project.

____

____

19. You're writing a letter to a local business to inquire about summer job opportunities. What information would you include in the body of the letter?

____

____

____

20. Imagine you're writing a letter to the mayor of your city to suggest improvements to your local park. What would be your main points in the body of the letter?

____

____

____

____

____

____

Writing Title

When writing the titles of books, publications, and movies and songs make sure that you use a capital letter of each word.

Squid Games   Star Trek   Grey's Anatomy   Finding Nemo

However, articles, prepositions, and conjunctions should not be capitalized unless it is the first letter.

Charlie and the Chocolate Factory   A Bronx Tale   Guardians of the Galaxy   The New York Times

When handwriting titles you should underline them, however when typing them they should be put into italics as seen above.

Poems, song titles, article, and chapter titles follow the same capitalization rules but instead of italics or underlining them, they should have quotation marks at the beginning and end.

"Permission to Dance"   "A Dream Deferred"   "Men Land on the Moon"   "The Letter"

Titles Practice:

Read each title carefully and determine if it is written correctly or if it contains errors. Circle "Correct" if the title is written properly. If there are errors, circle "Incorrect" rewrite the title correctly.

1. The Lion King (movie)
   Correct / Incorrect: ______________________________

2. To Kill a mockingbird (book)
   Correct / Incorrect: ______________________________

3. "Harry potter and the philosopher's stone" (book)
   Correct / Incorrect: ______________________________

4. the great gatsby (book)
   Correct / Incorrect: ______________________________

5. The Avengers: Endgame (movie)
   Correct / Incorrect: ______________________________

6. The Lord of the rings (book/movie)
   Correct / Incorrect: ______________________________

7. Titanic (movie)
   Correct / Incorrect: ______________________________

8. "thriller" by Michael Jackson (song)
   Correct / Incorrect: ______________________________

9. Avatar (movie)
   Correct / Incorrect: ______________________________

10. "hunger games" by Suzanne Collins (book)
    Correct / Incorrect:______________________________

11. Finding Nemo (movie)
Correct / Incorrect: ____________________

12. The Shawshank redemption (movie)
Correct / Incorrect: ____________________

13. "let it go" from Frozen (song)
Correct / Incorrect: ____________________

14. "the beatles: yellow submarine" (song)
Correct / Incorrect: ____________________

15. The Hobbit: An Unexpected Journey (book/movie)
Correct / Incorrect: ____________________

16. "The Catcher in the Rye" by J.D. Salinger
Correct / Incorrect: ____________________

17. "Bohemian Rhapsody" by Queen
Correct / Incorrect: ____________________

18. The Matrix
Correct / Incorrect: ____________________

19. "Beauty and the Beast"
Correct / Incorrect: ____________________

20. "Jurassic Park" by Michael Crichton
Correct / Incorrect: ____________________

Writing Dialogue

When you are writing about something that someone has said you should use quotation marks. The first word inside the quotation should be capitalized even if the quote comes at the end of the sentence.

Michael said, "The store is just around the corner."

Notice that the ending punctuation mark is also inside the quotation mark and before the quotation mark there is a comma.

She asked, "Do you have any orange juice?"

If the quotation comes at the beginning of the sentence replace a period with a comma but leave question marks.

"Do you know the Muffin Man?" she asked.
"Turn the music down," he said.

Quotations Practice: Put in the missing quotation marks.

Sarah and her little brother Jake ventured into the enchanted forest. In a magical clearing, a wise old owl perched on a branch. Who goes there? it hooted. Sarah and Jake replied, It's us, Sarah and Jake! The owl welcomed them and asked, What brings you here? Sarah explained, We're searching for the lost treasure of the forest. The owl nodded and said, I can show you the way, but the journey will be perilous. Are you brave enough? Sarah and Jake nodded eagerly. With the wise owl as their guide, they set off on their daring quest.

BOOK REVIEW

Read each sentence carefully. If there is a mistake, circle it and write the correction on the line. If it is correct, write "correct" on the line.

1. The cat purr loudly while sleeping. ____________________
2. She run quickly to catch the bus. ____________________
3. They're going to the zoo on May 15, 2023. ____________________
4. The red, juicy apple fell from the tree. ____________________
5. He draw a picture of his family. ____________________
6. We should of finished the project yesterday. ____________________
7. The weather is to cold for outdoor activities. ____________________
8. The teacher gave everyone a gold star. ____________________
9. The puppy wag it's tail happily. ____________________
10. They're favorite movie is "The Wizard of Oz". ____________________
11. My sister goed to the store to buy some groceries. ____________________
12. The big, brown dog barked loud in the park. ____________________
13. She is reading a interesting book about space. ____________________
14. The students' brought their lunches to school today. ____________________
15. Me and my friend went swimming at the pool. ____________________
16. The boy run fast to catch the baseball. ____________________

Rearrange the words to compose a correct sentence.

17. ran the children happily playground the in.

____

18. the house on cat roof the sat.

____

19. the sang loudly choir the in.

____

20. park they the played happily at.

____

21. homework afternoon did her yesterday.

____

22. the beach family happily walked the along.

____

23. dog wagged happily its tail the.

____

24. the bookshelf neatly arranged books on were the.

____

Read the sentence, circle the best word to complete the sentence.

25. The (big | bigger) dog barked loudly at the mailman.

26. We went to the zoo and saw two (elephant | elephants) playing.

27. Yesterday, my brother and I (run | ran) quickly to catch the bus.

28. The teacher asked us to bring our (book | books) to class tomorrow.

29. Sarah is reading a very (interesting | interested) book about space.

30. The (sunny | sunnier) weather is perfect for outdoor activities.

31. My mom baked delicious cookies in the (oven | ovens) last night.

32. He should have (finish | finished) his homework before going out to play.

33. The cat sleep (peaceful | peacefully) in the warm sunshine.

34. We're going to watch the movie "Frozen" with (they're | their) friends.

35. The (happy | happily) children played in the park all afternoon.

36. Yesterday, my sister and I (go | went) swimming at the pool.

37. The (brown | browned) bread smelled delicious as it toasted in the oven.

38. She is wearing a (pretty | prettily) dress for the party tonight.

39. The dog (wag | wagged) its tail eagerly when it saw its owner.

40. My favorite (movie | movies) is "The Lion King."

BOOK TEST

1. Identify the complete sentence:
   a) Running
   b) in the park
   c) Running in the park.

2. Choose the sentence that is a fragment:
   a) The dog barked loudly.
   b) On the table.
   c) She went to the store.

3. Identify the simple sentence:
"The cat chased the mouse."
   a) The cat chased
   b) The cat chased the mouse.
   c) The cat.

4. Choose the sentence that is a run-on:
   a) She walked to the store.
   b) She walked to the store, and she bought some milk.
   c) She walked to the store, she bought some milk.

5. Identify the compound sentence:
"She went to the store, and she bought some milk."
   a) She went to the store
   b) she bought some milk.
   c) She went to the store, and she bought some milk.

6. Choose the sentence that is a run-on:
   a) I like to play soccer, my favorite team is Real Madrid.
   b) I like to play soccer.
   c) My favorite team is Real Madrid.

7. Identify the common noun:
"The Eiffel Tower is in Paris."
   a) Eiffel Tower
   b) Paris
   c) The

8. Choose the singular form of the noun:
"geese"
   a) goose
   b) geese's
   c) gooses

9. Identify the proper noun:
"The cat chased the mouse."
   a) cat
   b) chased
   c) mouse

10. Choose the plural form of the noun:
"child"
   a) childs
   b) child's
   c) children

11. Identify the proper noun:
"The Statue of Liberty is in New York City."
   a) Statue
   b) Liberty
   c) New York City

12. Choose the plural form of the noun:
"box"
   a) boxes
   b) box's
   c) boxs

13. Choose the correct pronoun to complete the sentence: "My sister and __________ went to the park."

a) I
b) me
c) mine

14. Identify the relative pronoun:
"The book, which is on the table, is mine."

a) book
b) which
c) table

15. Choose the correct pronoun to complete the sentence:
"Sally and _______ went to the store."

a) she
b) her
c) they

16. Identify the reflexive pronoun:
"He hurt himself while playing."

a) He
b) hurt
c) himself

17. Choose the correct pronoun to complete the sentence: "My friends and ________ went to the movies."

a) me
b) I
c) my

18. Identify the reflexive pronoun:
"He hurt himself while playing."

a) He
b) hurt
c) himself

19. Choose the correct form of the verb:
"She ________ to the store yesterday."

a) go
b) goes
c) went

20. Identify the linking verb:
"The flowers smell wonderful."

a) flowers
b) smell
c) wonderful

21. Choose the correct form of the verb:
"They ________ to the beach every summer."

a) go
b) goes
c) went

22. Identify the action verb:
"The cat jumped onto the table."

a) cat
b) jumped
c) table

23. Choose the correct form of the adjective:
"This is the _________ day of my life."

a) happy
b) happier
c) happiest

24. Identify the adverb in the sentence:
"She speaks English fluently."

a) speaks
b) English
c) fluently

25. Choose the correct form of the adjective: "The sky is _________ today."

a) blue

b) bluer

c) bluest

26. Identify the adverb in the sentence: "He ran quickly to catch the bus."

a) ran

b) quickly

c) catch

27. Choose the sentence with the correctly placed comma in a list:

a) I like to eat apples oranges and bananas.

b) I like to eat apples, oranges, and bananas.

c) I like to eat apples oranges, and bananas.

28. Choose the sentence with the correctly placed comma for a date:

a) The event will take place on July 4 2022.

b) The event will take place on July 4, 2022.

c) The event will take place on July 4th 2022.

29. Choose the sentence with the correctly placed comma in a list:

a) He bought milk bread and eggs.

b) He bought milk, bread, and eggs.

c) He bought milk bread, and eggs.

30. Choose the sentence with the correctly placed comma for a date:

a) The event will take place on October 31st, 2024.

b) The event will take place on October 31, 2024.

c) The event will take place on October 31 2024.

31. Choose the sentence with the correctly placed comma for a location:

a) She lives in New York New York.

b) She lives in New York, New York.

c) She lives in New, York New York.

32. Choose the correct abbreviation for "Monday":

a) Mon.

b) Mndy.

c) Mondy.

33. Choose the correct abbreviation for "January":

a) Jan.

b) Jany.

c) Janr.

34. Choose the correct abbreviation for "Sunday":

a) Sun.

b) Sundy.

c) Suny.

35. Choose the correct greeting for a formal letter:

a) Hi,

b) Dear Sir or Madam,

c) Hey there,

36. Choose the correct closing for a formal letter:

a) Love,

b) Sincerely,

c) Best regards,

37. Choose the correct greeting for an informal letter:

a) Dear Sir or Madam,

b) Hi,

c) To whom it may concern,

38. Choose the correct closing for an informal letter:

a) Yours truly,

b) Best wishes,

c) Sincerely yours,

39. Choose the sentence with the correct use of quotation marks:

a) The teacher said that "the test is tomorrow."

b) The teacher said that "the test is tomorrow".

c) The teacher said that the test is tomorrow.

40. Choose the sentence with the correct use of quotation marks for direct speech:

a) She said, I am hungry.

b) She said, "I am hungry."

c) She said, I am hungry.

41. Choose the sentence with the correct use of quotation marks:

a) She said, "I am hungry."

b) She said, I am hungry.

c) She said "I am hungry."

42. Choose the sentence with the correct use of quotation marks for direct speech:

a) The teacher said that the test is tomorrow.

b) The teacher said that "the test is tomorrow."

c) The teacher said that the test is tomorrow.

스피킹 영역이 낮은 외고 1학년 G10학생

(eading, Writing, Speaking, Listening: basic)

- 어라운즈와 함께 준비한 기간: 2개월

이 학생은 외고를 재학 중인만큼 충분히 기본 베이스가 있었습니다. 단어도 많이 알았고 리딩문제 이해도는 상당히 높았습니다, 하지만 학년이 높았고 스피킹에 취약하여 개인의 상태에 맞는 커리큘럼으로 공부가 필요한 학생이었습니다. 공부적으로는 뛰어났으나 국제학교에서 요구하는 위기 대응 능력 순발력에서는 약점을 보였습니다. 그리고 당황하면 원어민 선생님의 말을 이해 못하는 경우도 있었습니다. 물론 원어민 선생님과의 접촉이 적어서 그럴 수도 있다고 생각했지만 국제학교 입시에 있어서는 정말로 중요한 부분에서 약점을 보였습니다. 라이팅도 써본 경험이 없어서 문단의 구조 및 아이디어를 내는 데서 어려움이 있었습니다.

- 어라운즈의 솔루션

이 학생의 경우 학년이 높았기 때문에 맵테스트와 SAT의 문법 부분을 섞어서 수업을 했습니다. SAT 문법 부분에서 필요한 부분만 발췌를 했고 MAP Test의 문학작품 부분에 집중을 했습니다. 스피킹의 경우 원어민 선생님과 함께 말하는 연습을 통해 어색함을 없애기 위해 노력을 하였습니다 그리고 말하는 것을 계속적으로 녹음 하였습니다. 녹음한 것을 들으면서 pronunciation, intonation (억양), 문법을 고쳐 나갔습니다. 언어는 습관이기 때문에 틀린 부분을 반복적으로 계속 고쳐 나갔습니다. 스피킹에서 쓰는 단어 실력을 높이기 위해 동의어 paraphrase 공부를 계속적으로 했고 그 단어가 스피킹에서 어떻게 쓰이는 지를 배웠습니다. 라이팅은 거의 하루에 250단어의 에세이를 2-3개 쓰도록 하였습니다. 선생님과 같이 첨삭하였고 아이디어의 고갈을 막기 위해 토픽 관련 리딩도 같이 진행을 했습니다. 학생은 잘 따라왔고 한번도 숙제를 안한적이 없습니다. 이 학생은 중국 미국 국제 학교에 고득점 (거의 만점)의 MAP 테스트를 받고 들어갈 수 있었습니다.

실력이 부족한 고2 학생 (11학년 지원)

(Reading, Writing, Speaking, Listening: Weak)

- 어라운즈와 함께 준비한 기간: 1개월

이 학생의 경우 실력은 부족하고 학년은 높았기 때문에 학교 선정부터 상당히 조심스러운 부분이 많았습니다. 시간 또한 1달로 충분하지 않았기 때문에 모의고사 위주로 준비하는 것에 집중해야 했습니다. 어느 한분야가 취약한 것이 아니라 전체적으로 취약했기 때문에 차근차근 해야 했고 영어에 대한 자신감이 없었습니다. 1달이라는 시간은 정말로 짧았으나 학생이 4시간 수업 및 4시간 자습을 통해 상당히 실력이 많이 늘었습니다.

- 어라운즈의 솔루션

짧은 준비 기간과 학생의 상태로 인해 반복적인 학습과 실전 연습을 해야 했습니다. 문제를 거의 외우다시피 할 정도로 같은 문제를 많이 풀며 문제 하나 하나에 대해 이해를 할 수 있도록 하였으며,9학년 부터 12학년 까지 준비를 시켰습니다. 또한 오답 노트를 쓰게 해서 왜 문제가 틀렸는지 분석하도록 하여 실전에 필요한 공부 위주로 학습했습니다. 하루에 4시간씩 수업을 했고 4시간 자습을 했습니다. 준비 기간은 짧았으나 인텐시브하게 공부를 시켰습니다. 짧은 시간 동안 많은 변화가 있었고 학생은 실력 향상이 빠르게 되었습니다. 이 학생은 제주 국제학교 BHA에 합격 할 수 있었습니다.

전체 영역이 낮은 G6 여학생

(Reading, Writing, Speaking, Listening: Weak)

- 어라운즈와 함께 준비한 기간: 6개월

이 학생의 경우 영어 공부를 늦게 시작했지만 의지가 있었던 학생이었습니다. 국제학교를 정말로 가기 희망했기 때문에 동기부여가 충분했습니다.

- 어라운즈의 솔루션

영어공부를 늦게 시작하여 맵테스트 점수는 낮았지만 스스로의 생각과 성향을 상대방이 파악할 수 있도록 이야기를 할 수 있다는 강점이 있었습니다.

가능성이 충분했기 때문에 단어를 정말로 열심히 외웠고, 기출문제 위주로 공부하며 부족한 맵테스트 점수를 보완할 수 있도록 지도했습니다. 목표가 확실했기 때문에 숙제나 단어 외우기에도 큰 열정을 보여 금방 성장할 수 있었습니다. 이 학생은 결국 가기 희망했던 비인가 국제학교에 합격하였습니다.

영어를 처음 시작한 G6 여학생

(Reading, Writing, Speaking, Listening: Weak)

- 어라운즈와 함께 준비한 기간: 6개월

이 학생은 특이한 케이스였습니다. 알파벳도 모르는 정도의 약점이 있었지만 성실함과 의지는 그 약점을 극복할 정도로 큰 강점을 가지고 있었습니다.

- 어라운즈의 솔루션

이 학생은 영어에 대한 이해가 거의 없었기 때문에 꾸준한 공부가 누구보다 중요했습니다. 스스로 성장하고자 하는 의지가 있었던 학생이기에 매일같이 어라운즈에서 공부를 했고, 단어 또한 상당히 많은 양을 외웠습니다. 알파벳부터 차근 차근 알려줘야 했기 때문에 기본기를 충분히 잡고 맵테스트 공부를 시작했습니다. 맵테스트와 함께 토플 공부를 하며 영어에 대해 더욱 깊이있고, 실용적으로 공부 할 수 있도록 지도했으며 원어민 선생님과 스피킹도 매일 꾸준히 진행했습니다. 한마디도 못하던 친구가 선생님과 대화를 하고 심지어 동생을 영어로 통역도 해주었습니다. 수학 공부도 영어로 진행을 하는 등 학생이 다양한 환경에서 학습을 할 수 있도록 지도했습니다. 이 학생은 6개월간 어라운즈와 준비하며 제주 BHA에 합격하였습니다.

ANSWER KEY

Pg. 7- Sentence Fragment

1) to music | The girl | listens | .

The girl listens to music.

2) Jenni | in a bunk bed | sleeps | .

Jenni sleeps in a bunk bed.

3) My mother | in the park | . | enjoys walking

My mother enjoys walking in the park.

4) . | are playing | The children | in the park

The children are playing in the park

5) in the kitchen | . | is | The dog

The dog is in the kitchen.

Pg. 8- Fix the Fragment

The lion ate	who	does	what/where
The lion ate an antelope. The lion ate in his den···			
caught fist	who	does	what/where
My grandpa caught a fish.			
My teacher	who	does	what/where
My teacher love coffee.			

Pg. 9- Sentence or Fragment

1.	He is my idol.	S	F
2.	I need a pen.	S	F
3.	The baton twirlers.	S	F
4.	The food is here.	S	F
5.	In the parade.	S	F
6.	Before the parade passes by.	S	F
7.	I don't know what to do.	S	F
8.	This is the way!	S	F
9.	Fire away!	S	F
10.	We are great friends.	S	F

Sentence writing- Answers will vary.

Pg. 10 Subject Practice: Underline the subject in each sentence.

Amanda likes to play soccer.

Ben wants to go to a soccer game.

Amanda and Ben will watch the Tottenham game this weekend!

They are playing against Chelsea.

The game starts at 3 o'clock.

Pg. 10- Complete the sentences by adding a subject to the given predicate.

(Answers my vary)

6)________ is Ben's favorite soccer player.

7)________ had a lot of fun at the game.

8)________ signed autographs after the game.

9)________was so excited when Sonny signed his jersey.

10)________ will remember this day forever!

Pg. 11- Predicate Practice

1. Jay is painting a tree.
2. Rachel is sitting in front of the tree.
3. Michael will meet them in the park later.
4. Jay will add Rachel and Michael to his painting.
5. He wants to be a painter in the future.

Add a predicate to complete the sentence.

Answers vary

6. Vincent Van Gogh ________________.
7. He________________.
8. Many people ________________.
9. Starry Night ________________.
10. Painting ________________.

Pg. 12- Sentence & Command Practice: Read the sentence. If it is a statement sentence circle S if it is a command, circle C.

Open the door.	S	C
My sister likes Mac and Cheese.	S	C
Eat your vegetables.	S	C
Flowers bloom in spring.	S	C
I haven't read that book.	S	C
Don't write in the book!	S	C
He is a very good dancer.	S	C
Practice your scales.	S	C
Tell me about your family.	S	C
That is a really good book.	S	C

pg. 13- Question Practice: Fill in the blank with the correct Wh Word and answer the question for yourself.

7) When is your birthday? My birthday is ________.

8) What is your age? I am ____ years old.

8) What is your father's name? My father's name is _____.

9) Who is sitting next to you? ____ is sitting next to me.

10) Why are you learning English? I'm learning English ____.

11) Where do you live? I live in Korea.

Pg. 14- Yes/No Answer Practice: Answer the question about you and your family.

1. Have you been to America? Answers Vary
2. Do you like broccoli? Answers Vary
3. Do you have a sister? Answers Vary
4. Do you like Indian food? Answers Vary
5. Have you tried escargot? Answers Vary

Pg. 14 Yes/No Question Practice: Write the question asked based on the answer given.

6. Do you like cheesecake? Yes, I like cheesecake.
7. Have you been to Africa? No, I haven't been to Africa.
8. Do you have a cat? No, I don't have a cat.
9. Do you like Sci-fi movies? Yes, I like Sci-fi movies.
10. Do you like poetry? No, I don't like poetry.

Pg. 15- Punctuation Practice

1.	Are you hungry	?	!
2.	I love chocolate	?	!
3.	Do you speak Spanish	?	!
4.	SURPRISE	?	!
5.	Sonny was here	?	!
6.	Where is the remote	?	!
7.	I'm the king of the world	?	!
8.	Where does he live	?	!
9.	Would you like to go to the movies	?	!
10.	That's my favorite movie	?	!

Pg. 16- Sentence Type Review:

C-B-A-B-C
C-A-A

Pg. 17- Conjunction Practice

1. I want to eat pizza or spaghetti for dinner.
2. Sarah wants to play soccer and/or tennis this weekend.
3. He likes to read books and watch movies in his free time.
4. The weather is cold, but we're still going to the park.
5. Would you like chocolate or vanilla ice cream for dessert?
6. She studied hard, so she passed the test with flying colors.
7. He is allergic to peanuts, so he cannot eat peanut butter sandwiches.
8. We can go to the beach or visit the zoo tomorrow.

Pg. 19- Compound Sentence Practice

1. I like ketchup but I don't like tomatoes.	C	S
2. My favorite food is pizza.	C	S
3. There are open seats in the front or you can stand in the back.	C	S
4. All the world's a stage.	C	S
5. Mint Chocolate is the worst ice cream flavor.	C	S

Pg. 19- Use the given word and to make compound sentences.

1	but	The market is open on Sundays. It isn't open on holidays. The market is open on Sundays but isn't open on holidays.
2	and	She likes BTS. She also likes the Beach Boys. She likes BTS and the Beach Boys.
3	or	Do you want to go to a movie? Do you want to have dinner first? Do you want to go to a movie or have dinner first?
4	but	I wanted to go to the concert. The tickets were sold out. I wanted to go to the concert but the tickets were sold out.
5	so	It's expensive to go to Europe. I saved for a year. It's expensive to go to Europe, so I saved for a year.

Pg. 21- Run On Sentence Practice:

5) Blue whales are the largest animals in the world very gentle.

Separate: Blue whales are the largest animals in the world. They are very gentle.

Conj (and): Blue whales are the largest animals in the world and are very gentle.

6) Mosquitos are one of the smallest animals the most dangerous.

Separate: Mosquitos are one of the smallest animals. Mosquitos are the most dangerous animals.

Conj (but): Mosquitos are one of the smallest animals but the most dangerous.

7) I have a pet rabbit I buy a lot of carrots.

Separate: I have a pet rabbit. I buy a lot of carrots.

Conj (so): I have a pet rabbit so I buy a lot of carrots.

8) Hamsters are tiny animals they make good pets.

Separate: Hamsters are tiny animals. They make good pets.

Conj (so): Hamsters are tiny animals so they make good pets.

Pg.22- Sentence Review:
Read the phrases below. If it is a complete sentence circle S, if it is a fragment circle F and if it is a run-on circle R.

I really like Mexican food.	S	F	R
Tacos are delicious.	S	F	R
I ate too much cake now I'm sick.	S	F	R
My mom makes great japchae.	S	F	R
I can't.	S	F	R
We have to clean my grandparents are coming.	S	F	R
My grandma's birthday.	S	F	R
I painted a picture for my grandma.	S	F	R
I painted her favorite flowers I hope she likes it.	S	F	R
I'll give it to her at the party.	S	F	R

Read the paragraph and fix the fragment and run on sentences. (3)

Yesterday, I went to the park with my friends. We Played on the swings. Then, we had a picnic with sandwiches and juice. After that, we played soccer until it was time to go home. It was so much fun. We saw a big rainbow in the sky. It was colorful and beautiful. We also found a caterpillar crawling on a leaf. I wanted to keep it as a pet but my mom said we had to let it go. I hope we can go to the park again soon.

Pg.23-24- Put the words in the correct order to make a complete sentence.

very hot | It | is | .	It is very hot.
the weather today | is | What | ?	What is the weather today?
Let's | ! | to the beach | go	Let's go to the beach!
forget | don't | to wear | ! | sunblock	Don't forget to wear sunblock!
swim | in the ocean | ? | Can you	Can you swim in the ocean?
sharks | ! | out for | Look	Look out for sharks!
the best day ever | was | Today | !	Today was the best day ever!

My mother	are beautiful.
The children	makes us dinner every night.
I	want to be an astronaut.
My cat	is swimming in the lake.
A duck	are playing in the park.
The flowers	had kittens this weekend.

My mother makes us dinner every night.

The children are playing in the park.

I want to be an astronaut.

My cat had kittens this weekend.

A duck is swimming in the lake.

The flowers are beautiful.

Pg.25- Read the sentence and circle the correct type of sentence. S for statement, C for command, Q for question, and E for exclamation.

1.	Have you ever been to Rome?	S	C	Q	E
2.	Everyone should go at least once.	S	C	Q	E
3.	Beware of pickpockets!	S	C	Q	E
4.	Rome is beautiful!	S	C	Q	E
5.	The food is amazing.	S	C	Q	E
6.	Millions of people visit Rome every year.	S	C	Q	E

Pg.25- Fix the run on sentence.

1. It's going to rain take an umbrella.

It's going to rain so take an umbrella.

2. It may be expensive I want to go to New York.

It may be expensive but I want to go to New York.

3. My mom's birthday is tomorrow I need to buy flowers.

My mom's birthday is tomorrow so I need to buy flowers.

4. Marcia has a brother Jessica has a sister.

Marcia has a brother and Jessica has a sister.

5. Spain is very laid back Italy is very busy.

Spain is very laid back but Italy is very busy.

Pg.26-28- Sentence Test

1. a) Simple
2. b) Compound
3. c) Complex
4. c) Complex
5. c) until
6. b) because
7. a) Run-on sentence
8. b) Fragment
9. a) Run-on sentence
10. b) Fragment
11. "I want pizza, I am hungry."
12. "Running around the park is fun."
13. "She loves to swim, but he prefers to hike."
14. "After the rain stopped, we went outside."
15. Compound sentence
16. Complex sentence
17. Simple sentence
18. Compound sentence
19. b) because
20. c) and
21. "They played soccer, and the sun was shining."
22. "After the storm passed, we went outside."
23. "She enjoys painting, and he likes to play the guitar."
24. "The birds chirped loudly while the sun rose in the sky."
25. Simple sentence

Pg. 33- Noun Practice: Read the story below. Circle the common nouns and underline the proper nouns.

My grandmother likes to visit her friend Margie. She will go to her house and sit on the porch drinking lemonade. Sometimes, they play games like Go Fish or Crazy Eights. My grandmother takes her dog Mimi. Mimi is a Pomeranian. She sits under my grandmother's chair sleeping. Grandma can't visit today because Margie is in Mexico visiting her sister.

Practice: Complete the chart Answers my vary

Common	Proper Noun
school	Harvard
girl	Angel
boy	Brian
store	E-Mart
restaurant	McDonalds

Common Noun	Proper Noun
teacher	Lauren T.
song	Baby Shark
movie	Fast X
soda	Coca Cola
book	Matilda

Pg. 34- Capitalization Practice

1. my sister's name is angela.

My sister's name is Angela.

2. one day, i want to visit the grand canyon.

One day, I want to visit the Grand Canyon.

3. we got burgers from mcdonalds.

We got burgers from Mcdonalds.

4. my father is a professor at yale university.

My father is a professor at Yale University.

5. i've been to disneyland in california, tokyo, and shanghai.

I've been to Disneyland in California, Tokyo, and Shanghai.

6. I'm going to the movies with francesca and marco on sunday.

I'm going to the movies with Francesca and Marco on Sunday,

Pg. 35- A/An Practice: Read and circle a or an.

1.)	a / an	alien
2.)	a / an	cat
3.)	a / an	elephant
4.)	a / an	gold coin
5.)	a / an	ice cube
6.)	a / an	kangaroo

7.)	a / an	ball
8.)	a / an	dragon
9.)	a / an	fish
10.)	a / an	hero
11.)	a / an	juice box
12.)	a / an	lion

Pg. 36- Article Practice:

1. Do you want to go to the zoo this weekend?
2. Sure, but is there a panda habitat?
3. Yes, but the pandas are usually hiding.
4. I wanted to take a picture with them.
5. You can take a picture with an elephant.
6. I'm afraid of the elephants!
7. My teacher volunteered at a sanctuary for elephants in Thailand.
8. She said the volunteers had a lot of fun.
9. She even fed one elephant a banana.

Pg. 38- Plural Noun Practice: look and write -s or -es to make the singular noun plural.

1.	computers	1.	toys
2.	bushes	2.	bottles
3.	carts	3.	chickens
4.	foxes	4.	shoes
5.	benches	5.	glassees

Practice: Complete the sentence with the correct form of the word.

1. [berry] I had a cup of mixed berries with lunch.
2. [shelf] Put the book on the shelves.
3. [elf] Have you ever wondered how Santa found the elves.
4. [city] Did you visit many cities in Italy?

Pg. 39- Irregular Plural Nouns: Look and write

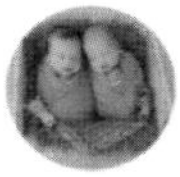
babies

tomatoes

apples
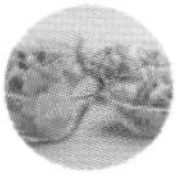
candy

wolves

brushes

Pg. 40- Count & Uncountable Nouns Practice:

1. We had spaghetti **| spaghettis** for dinner.
2. There are **monkey |** monkeys in the trees.
3. We volunteered to pick up trash **| trashes** this weekend.
4. I have to take these **book |** books back to the library.
5. I like Four Cheese **| Cheeses** pizza.
6. May we have three **hamburger |** hamburgers, please?
7. We drank some orange juice **| juices** after the game.
8. There are **oxes |** oxen in the field.
9. I will make some rice **| rices** for dinner.

Pg. 41- Count/Noncount Nouns and Articles Practice: Write the correct article (a, an, the, some, any) to complete the sentence.

1. There is a sandwich on the table.
2. There are some bananas in the bag.
3. May I have some juice?
4. There aren't any olives in the salad.
5. Is there a/any salad on the menu?
6. I need a pencil.
7. There's an elephant in my pajamas.
8. Keep an eye on the clock.
9. Do you want to see a movie?
10. I really need a/some coffee.

Pg. 42- Possessive Noun Practice: Write the noun in the possessive form.

7) Michael	Michael's	10) Jason	Jason's
8) The dog	the dog's	11) Teacher	Teacher's
9) The girls	the girl's	12_ Lisa	Lisa's

Pg. 43- Complete the sentence with the possessive noun.

1. [Marsha] The ball hit Marsha's nose.
2. [cows] We cleaned the cows' stalls.
3. [gardener] You'll find a rake in the gardener's shed.
4. [batter] Baez is practicing in the batter's cage.
5. [Jennie] Have you heard Jennie's new song?
6. [mom] I really miss my mom's cooking.
7. [girls] These are girls' shoes.
8. [fly] The boy plucked the fly's wings.
9. [sister] I helped curl my sister's hair for the party.
10. [Greg] That is Greg's bike.

Pg. 43- Read the sentence, if there is a mistake, circle it and write the correction on the line. If it is correct, write "correct".

11. Have you seen the baby's clothes?	Correct
12. I need to borrow Michaels' computer.	Michael's
13. These are the boys' jeans.	Correct or boy's
14. Turn off the lightes before bed.	lights
15. I'm looking for my dads glasses.	dad's
16. These are cat's toys.	Correct

Pg. 44- Noun Review

Circle **the nouns in the paragraph.**

Once upon a time there was a beautiful princess, named Cinderella. She lived with her stepmother and two sisters. They were not kind to Cinderella and made her clean the ashes, which is how she got her name. One day a kind fairy helped to send her to a ball held by the king and queen to help their son find a wife. Prince Christopher fell in love with Cinderella right away. They were married and lived happily ever after.

Pg. 44- Read the sentence. If there is a mistake, circle it and make the correction on the line. If the sentence is correct, write "Correct" on the line.

17. My name is marsha brady. Marsha
18. Tiffany went to harvard University. Harvard
19. I want Burger King for dinner. Correct
20. The panda had two babys. babies
21. I had an sandwich for lunch. a sandwich
22. There are a lot of people here. correct
23. There aren't any childrens in the park. children
24. She has an apple computer. Apple

Pg. 45-48- Noun Test

1. c) tree
2. b) summer
3. a) books
4. a) mouse
5. b) A
6. c) The
7. c) advice
8. c) cars
9. b) dog's
10. b) children's
11. c) knives
12. a) person
13. a) Statue of Liberty
14. c) park
15. c) The
16. a) An
17. c) milk
18. c) clouds
19. b) cat's
20. b) teacher's
21. c) boxes
22. c) toy
23. b) Paris
24. c) school
25. a) An

Pg. 51- Pronouns

Read the story below. Circle all of the nouns.

Michael is excited. **Michael** is going to **Michael's grandmother's house** this **weekend**. **Michael's grandmother** lives on a **farm**. **Michael** is very excited to feed the **cows** and **chickens**. **Michael** will also go fishing with **Michael's grandfather**. If **Michael** and **Michael's grandfather** catch a **fish**, **Michael's grandmother** will cook the **fish** for **dinner**. **Michael**, **Michael's grandmother**, and **Michael's grandmother** can't wait for **Michael's visit**.

How many times is Michael's name written? 14

Pg. 52- Pronoun Practice: Read the story and replace the highlighted nouns with the correct subject pronoun.

Jasmine wanted to go to the party. The party was for Brian's birthday. Brian[1] would have chocolate cake. Jasmine[2] wanted to find the perfect present for Brian. Jasmine went to three stores before Jasmine[3] found one. Brian loved dinosaurs. Brian[4] would like the dinosaur game that Jasmine found. The game had a dinosaur theme. Maybe Jasmine and Brian[5] could play the game[6] together.

1) He	2) She	3) She
4) He	5) they	6) it

Pg. 53- Object Pronoun Practice: Read the sentences. Circle the subjects and underline the object.

1. **She** likes ice cream.
2. **He** went to the store.
3. **We** are going on a picnic.
4. **I** recently read The Hobbit.
5. **It** is cold outside.
6. Are **you** hungry?
7. **They** are watching a movie.

Pg. 53- Practice: Write the correct object pronoun. Circle the subject noun it replaces.

8. I really like cookies. I could eat **them** everyday.
9. Jack chased Jill up the hill. She chased **him** after.
10. There is a cake on the table. Please don't touch **it** .
11. Lauren is on the phone. Do you want to talk to **her**.
12. I got a gold medal yesterday. My school gave it to **me**.

Pg. 54- Subject and Object Pronoun Review

Complete the sentence with the correct pronoun.

10) I like coffee and tea.

11) She is the girl in the blue dress.

12) Do you like to go hiking?

13) He asked his mom to give him ice cream.

14) We/They are going to the movies after dinner.

15) Can you bring those books to me?

16) Maria's brother picks her up from school everyday.

17) My brother loves the video game I gave him.

18) Our teacher is going to tell us who won the science competition.

Pg. 54- Choose the correct sentence.

1.

a.) Tree climb you?

b.) Can you climb a tree?

2.

a.) We all have iPhones except she.

b.) We all have iPhones except her.

3.

a.) Us had a picnic in the park?

b.) We had a picnic in the park?

4.

a.) He has a big test tomorrow.

b.) Him has a big test tomorrow.

5.

a.) Her is going to Spain this year.

b.) She is going to Spain this year.

Pg. 55- Possessive pronouns

Practice: Fill in the blank with the correct possessive pronoun.

Ex. I bought these cookies. They are mine.

1. Peter and Mary got new bikes. These are theirs.
2. I don't have a pen, can I borrow yours?
3. This shirt belongs to John. It is his.
4. Jessica let me borrow a cup, this is hers.
5. We just got a new car. The blue one is ours.
6. If these are your shoes, where are mine?

Pg. 55- Read the sentence. If there is a mistake, circle it and make the correction on the line. If the sentence is correct, write "Correct" on the line.

1. Come to our house for dinner. Correct
2. My sister lives in Spain? My sister lives in Spain.
3. Is this you pencil? your

Pg. 56- Relative Pronoun Practice: Circle the relative pronouns in the sentence in sentence.

1. Can you pass me the cup that's on the table?
2. I'm the one who made the cake.
3. I found a dress which I love!
4. Let's go someplace where we've never been before!
5. You can invite whomever you like to the party.

Pg. 58- Reflexive Pronoun Practice: Choose the sentence that is written correctly.

1.)	Help yourself to some popcorn.	Help youself to some popcorn.	Help you to some popcorn.
2.)	The baby can feed hiself.	The baby can feed himself.	The baby can feed heself.
3.)	I made my dress meself.	I made my dress myself.	I made my dress Iself.
4.)	She can buy flowers for herself.	She can buy flowers for sheself.	She can buy flowers himself.
5.)	We can seat ourselves.	We can seat ourselfs.	We can seat usselves.

Pg. 58- Read the sentence. If there is a mistake, circle it and make the correction on the line. If the sentence is correct, write "Correct" on the line.

1. I can move the couch myself. Correct
2. She's not afraid to travel by himself. herself
3. Dad made dinner himself. Correct
4. Cats lick itself clean. themselves
5. The horse can get home itself. Correct
6. He put myself through school. himself
7. I'm too tired to cook dinner for herself. myself
8. They locked themselves out of the house. correct

Pg. 59-60- Pronoun Review
Read the paragraph and circle the pronouns.

Once, two kids, Alex and Emily, got stuck in a candy store. They looked everywhere but couldn't find a way out. They felt hungry and scared. Then, the store owner came back, unlocked the door, and let them go. They were happy to be free again after their candy store adventure. They promised to be more careful next time they went exploring.

Fill in the blank with the correct pronoun.

1. **I/he/she they/ we** went to the store to buy some apples.
2. She gave **him** a present for his birthday.
3. The book **he/she** is reading is very interesting.
4. That's John, **he** is the tallest student in the class.
5. I saw a movie by **myself** last night.
6. The teacher asked **them** to turn in their homework.
7. They couldn't find **their** keys.
8. The dog, **who/that** barks loudly, chased the cat up a tree.
9. Sarah, **who** is my best friend, invited me to her birthday party.
10. The children **who** built the sandcastle at the beach were proud of their creation.

1. Him went to the store to buy some candy.	he
2. She gave me a present for his birthday.	him
3. The book her is reading is very interesting.	she
4. Him is the tallest student in the class.	he
5. I saw a movie with she last night.	her

Choose the correct sentence.

1.)	Her went to the park with his friends.	She went to the park with his friends.	She went to the park with her friends.
2.)	Me loves to play with he at recess.	I loves to play with him at recess.	I love to play with him at recess.
3.)	Him ate all of the cookies by he.	He ate all of the cookies by him.	He ate off of the cookies by himself.
4.)	They picked up she after school.	Them picked up her after school.	They picked her up after school.
5.)	We made a card for they.	US made a card for them.	We made a card for them.

Pg. 61-63- Pronouns Test

1. c) He
2. a) We
3. d) They
4. a) He
5. b) They
6. c) Her
7. b) Her
8. d) Him
9. b) Him
10. b) Her
11. d) Himself
12. c) Herself
13. d) Himself
14. c) Themselves
15. c) Yourself
16. b) She
17. d) Them
18. b) He
19. b) They
20. d) Us

Pg. 68- Verbs Practice: Draw a square around the verb.

1. The cat sleeps peacefully on the windowsill.
2. Sarah dances ballet every Saturday.
3. The sun shines brightly in the sky.
4. Max runs quickly in the race.
5. The birds sing sweetly in the morning.

Practice: Put the sentence in order.

1. jumps / the / happily / dog / up / and / down

The dog jumps up and down happily.

2. in / the / my / park / friends / play / and / I

My friends and I play in the park.

3. eats / the / lunch / squirrel / in / the / tree

The squirrel eats lunch in the tree.

4. sings / the / sweetly / bird / morning / in / the

The bird sings sweetly in the morning.

Pg. 71- Be Verbs Practice: Fill in the blank with the correct be verb.

1. Sarah is happy when she plays with her friends.
2. The sky is blue on a sunny day.
3. My cat is sleeping on the couch.
4. The flowers are blooming in the garden.
5. The book is interesting to read.
6. The dog is barking at the mailman.
7. My mom is cooking dinner in the kitchen.
8. The stars are shining brightly in the night sky.
9. The baby is laughing and giggling.
10. Our teacher is kind and helpful to us.

Pg. 73- Present Simple Practice: Complete the sentence with the provided verb correctly.

1. Sarah plays (play) soccer with her friends after school.
2. The birds sing (sing) beautifully in the trees every morning.
3. My mom cooks (cook) dinner for our family in the evening.
4. The sun shines (shine) brightly in the sky during the day.
5. Max and Emily study (study) together for their math test.
6. The cat sleeps (sleep) peacefully on the windowsill.
7. We visit (visit) Grandma and Grandpa on Sundays.
8. The flowers bloom (bloom) in the garden during the spring.
9. Dad drives (drive) us to school every morning.
10. The teacher teaches (teach) us new lessons every day.
11. Alex reads (read) his favorite book before bedtime.
12. The dog barks (bark) loudly whenever someone knocks on the door.

Read the sentence. If there is a mistake, circle it and make the correction on the line. If the sentence is correct, write "Correct" on the line.

1. Sarah play soccer after school.	plays
2. The birds sing every morning.	correct
3. My mom cooking dinner for our family in the evening.	cooks
4. The sun shines brightly in the sky during the night.	moon/ day

Pg. 74- Present Simple Irregular Practice: Fill in the blank with the correct usage of the given verb.

1. Sarah does (do) her homework every day after school.
2. Max and Emily go (go) to the park on weekends.
3. The cat takes (take) a nap in the afternoon sun.
4. We have (have) pizza for dinner on Fridays.
5. Mom goes (go) to work early in the morning.

Pg. 77- Irregular Present Continuous Practice: Write the word correctly in Present Progressive tense.

1. Swim: swimming	9. Write: writing
2. Run: running	10. Sing: singing
3. Play: playing	11. Paint: painting
4. Dance: dancing	12. Laugh: laughing
5. Read: reading	13. Study: studying
6. Jump: jumping	14. Talk: talking
7. Sleep: sleeping	15. Cook: cooking
8. Eat: eating	16. Climb: climbing

1. Sarah is playing with her friends at the playground.
2. The dog is jumping in the backyard.
3. Max and Emily are running in the park.
4. The cat is sleeping on the windowsill.
5. We are eating pizza for dinner tonight.
6. The children are laughing and having fun at the party.

Pg. 78- Present Continuous Review:

Read the sentence, if there are any mistakes, circle it and write the correction on the line. If it is correct, write "Correct" on the line.

1. Sarah am going to the store.	is going
2. The birds sing in the trees.	correct
3. Max and Emily is playing soccer.	are playing
4. Mom are cooking dinner in the kitchen.	is
5. We are eat lunch at school.	are eating
6. The dog sleeps on the couch.	Correct
7. Dad is reads a book in the living room.	reading
8. The children is running in the park.	are running
9. The cat are sleeping on the bed.	is
10. The students are study for their test.	studying

Choose the correct word to complete the sentence.

11. Sarah and her brother (is | are) building a sandcastle at the beach.
12. The teacher (teaches | teaching) a lesson in the classroom.
13. The baby (is | are) crawling on the floor.
14. We (are | being) watching a movie at home.
15. The birds (fly | flying) high in the sky.

Pg. 79- Present Simple vs Present Progressive Review

Read the paragraph below. Use the verbs in the box to correctly complete the story.

read	sleep	chase	go	sing
cook	play	watch	bloom	shine

In the morning, the sun (1) shines brightly in the sky, and the birds (2) sing sweetly in the trees. Sarah (3) is reading her favorite book on the porch while her mom (4) cook breakfast. Max and Emily (5) are playing with their toys, and the cat (6) is sleeping on the couch. Dad (7) watches TV before he (8) goes to work. Outside, the flowers (9) are blooming in the garden, and the dog (10) is chasing its tail.

Choose the correct word to complete the sentence.

11. Sarah usually (reads/reading) a book before bedtime.
12. Right now, the kids (play/ are playing) in the backyard.
13. The flowers (bloom/blooming) beautifully in the garden every spring.
14. Max often (watches/watching) his favorite cartoons on Saturday mornings.
15. Look! The cat (sleeps/is sleeping) peacefully on the windowsill.

Pg. 82- Practice: Read the passage below. Circle all of the past tense verbs.

Yesterday, I visited the zoo. I wanted to see all the different animals. I looked at a penguin with an orange beak. I asked the zookeeper where they sleep. I learned that they stayed on the ice to sleep. I enjoyed spending the day watching as the penguins marched around their habitat. Later, I imitated them and walked home.

Pg. 82- Practice: Choose the correct word from the box to complete the sentence by writing the verb correctly.

visit	run	chase	read	sing
cook	play	watch	shine	paint

1. Yesterday, Sarah played soccer with her friends.
2. Max and Emily visited their grandparents last weekend.
3. The cat chased a mouse around the house.
4. Dad cooked dinner for the family yesterday.
5. We watched a movie at the cinema last night.
6. The birds sang beautifully in the trees this morning.
7. Mom read a bedtime story to us last night.
8. The dog ran around the park with its owner.
9. Sarah painted a picture in art class yesterday.
10. The sun shone brightly during our picnic yesterday.

Pg. 83- Practice Past Irregular Verbs: Write the verbs correctly to complete the journal entry.

Dear Diary,

Today was an exciting day! In the morning, I (1) woke (wake) up early because I (2) had (have) a big test at school. After breakfast, I (3) ran (run) to catch the bus, but I (4) missed (miss) it! So, I (5) walked (walk) to school instead. During the test, I (6) wrote (write) down all the answers carefully. Afterward, my friends and I (7) went (go) to the park for a picnic lunch. We (8) ate (eat) sandwiches and played games until it started to rain. When I (9) arrived (arrive) home, I (10) did (do) my homework and then (11) had (have) dinner with my family.

I'm tired now, but it was a great day overall!
Love, Diana

Pg. 85- Past tense review.

1. Sarah plays soccer every Saturday morning.
2. Right now, the kids are playing in the garden.
3. Max visited his grandparents last weekend.
4. Mom is cooking dinner for the family right now.
5. We usually watch a movie at home on Fridays.
6. The birds sing beautifully in the trees every morning.
7. Dad read a book in the living room last night.
8. The dog is running around the park with its owner.
9. Sarah painted a picture in art class yesterday.
10. The sun shone brightly during our picnic yesterday.
11. Sarah and her brother are playing in the yard right now.
12. Last summer, we visited the beach with our friends.
13. The cat slept on the couch all day yesterday.
14. Mom baked cookies for us in the kitchen.
15. Right now, I am reading a book in my room.

Pg. 86- Future Tense Practice
Find the future tense verbs in the story and circle them.

My name is Jessica,
and when I grow up, I want to be a doctor.
As a doctor, I will help sick people feel better. I will check their heartbeats, take their temperature, and give them medicine to help them get well. I will need to study hard in school to learn about the human body and how to treat different illnesses.
I will also need to go to medical school after I finish high school.
In medical school, I will learn even more about being a doctor.
I will work in a hospital or a clinic, and I will wear a white coat and a stethoscope around my neck. I can't wait to become a doctor and help people every day!

Pg. 88-90- Verb Review

1. a) am
2. c) present simple
3. d) went
4. b) playing
5. c) "They will be playing basketball after school."
6. d) present simple
7. d) ate
8. b) reads
9. c) "We are watching a movie right now."
10. b) present simple
11. b) swam
12. c) writing
13. c) "She danced at the party last night."
14. a) present simple
15. c) runs
16. b) drank
17. c) "He reads books every day."
18. b) past simple
19. c) slept
20. b) studying
21. c) "She danced at the party last night."
22. a) present simple
23. c) spoke
24. a) watch

Pg. 93- Modal Verb Practice
Fill in the blank with the correct modal verb. Some sentences could have multiple answers.

1. should - You should eat vegetables to stay healthy.
2. can - We can go to the park if it's sunny.
3. should - Sarah should help her friend with homework.
4. should - I should drink milk to make my bones strong.
5. must - Max must clean his room before he plays.
6. should - You should ask for help if you don't understand.
7. will - The teacher will read a story to the class.
8. will - Mom will bake cookies for us this weekend.
9. should - The cat should sleep in its bed at night.
10. should - We should say "please" and "thank you" to be polite.
11. must - You must wear a helmet when riding a bike.
12. can - Sarah can play with her toys after finishing her homework.
13. should - We should listen to our parents to stay safe.
14. can - The birds can sing sweetly in the morning.
15. will - I will help my friend when they are sad.

Pg. 95- Present Perfect Practice

1. has finished - Sarah has finished her homework.
2. have visited - We have visited the zoo.
3. has cleaned - Max has cleaned his room.
4. has eaten - The cat has eaten its food.
5. has cooked - Mom has cooked dinner for us.
6. have played - They have played soccer.
7. have read - I have read a book.
8. have done - You have done your chores.
9. has built - He has built a sandcastle.
10. has painted - She has painted a picture.
11. have not forgotten - We have not forgotten to feed the fish.
12. have not seen - They have not seen the movie yet.
13. Has Sarah finished - Has Sarah finished her project?
14. Have you cleaned - Have you cleaned your room yet?

Pg. 96- Past Perfect Practice: Correct the sentences below or write "correct" if there are no corrections to make.

1. Sarah had went to bed early last night. gone
2. Max had did his homework before dinner. done
3. Mom had cook dinner when we arrived. cooked
4. They had saw a movie after school. seen
5. I had finished my project before the deadline. correct
6. You had not did your chores yet. done
7. He had went to the store yesterday. gone
8. We had visited our grandparents last weekend. Correct
9. She had not went to the park with her friends. gone

Pg. 97- Past Perfect Practice: Correct the sentences below or write "correct" if there are no corrections to make.

1. Sarah had went to bed early last night. gone
2. Max had did his homework before dinner. done
3. Mom had cook dinner when we arrived. cooked
4. They had saw a movie after school. seen
5. I had finished my project before the deadline. correct
6. You had not did your chores yet. done
7. He had went to the store yesterday. gone
8. We had visited our grandparents last weekend. Correct
9. She had not went to the park with her friends. gone

Pg. 98- Future Perfect Tense Practice

By the time I finish school next year, I will have completed (complete) my project. My family and I will have moved (move) to a new house by then. We will have lived (live) in our current home for ten years. My parents will have bought (buy) the new house last month. By the time we move, we will have packed (pack) all our belongings.

Pg. 100 Perfect Tense Review

1. b) "By next summer, I will have planted flowers in the garden."
2. c) ate
3. b) played
4. c) "She has read three books this month."
5. b) swam
6. b) wrote
7. c) "She has finished her homework already."
8. d) will have studied
9. b) sang
10. c) "By next month, we will have finished the project."
11. b) drank
12. b) slept
13. c) "She has painted three pictures this week."
14. d) will have run
15. b) spoke
16. d) "We have finished our homework."
17. d) will have written
18. b) swam
19. c) "She has finished her painting."
20. d) will have danced
21. b) slept
22. c) "She has cooked dinner already."
23. d) will have studied
24. b) ate

Pg. 101-Subject verb agreement practice
Read the paragraph and find the six mistakes in subject verb agreement. Correct them in the paragraph.

A group of friendly animals live in the forest. Every morning, they wake up and goes **go** for a walk together. The rabbit hops ahead, while the squirrel scurry **scurries** beside. The birds sing happily as they fly overhead. Suddenly, they hears **hear** a loud noise. They stops **stop** and listen carefully. It sounds like thunder. The animals gets **get** scared and run back to their homes. When the storm pass **passes**, they come out again to play. They knows **know** that as long as they stick together, they can face anything.

Verb Review
Read the story below and underline all the verbs you find.

Once upon a time, there was a curious cat named Whiskers. Every day, Whiskers would explore the neighborhood, chase butterflies, and climb trees. One day, Whiskers discovered a hidden path in the woods. Excitedly, Whiskers followed the path and found a magical garden at the end.

Fill in the blank with the given verb in the correct tense.

1. Sarah is playing (play) with her toys in the room now.
2. We finished (finish) our project next week.
3. The birds sing (sing) sweetly in the morning.
4. Yesterday, Max rode (ride) his bike in the park.
5. By the time we arrive, they will have prepared (prepare) dinner.

Read the sentence below, if there is a mistake circle it and write the correction on the line. If there is no mistake write "Correct"

1. She is dance in the living room. dancing
2. They has went to the beach last summer. had gone
3. He will reads a book tomorrow. read
4. Yesterday, we have went to the zoo. went
5. By next month, they have finished the puzzle. will have

Pg. 103- Use the words from the word bank to complete the sentence correctly

must could may might should

1. You should/must eat vegetables to stay healthy.
2. Sarah could help her friend with homework yesterday.
3. We must/should say "please" and "thank you" to be polite.
4. May I have a glass of water?
5. Next summer, my family might travel to Europe.

Pg. 103- Fill in the blanks with the correct be verb.

1. She is going to the store.
2. They are happy with their new toys.
3. The cat is sleeping on the couch.
4. We are going to the park tomorrow.
5. He is my best friend.

Pg. 104-106- Verbs Test

1. a) am
2. c) They are playing in the park.
3. b) is
4. a) plays
5. c) We play games at the party.
6. b) flies
7. c) running
8. c) are playing
9. c) is sleeping
10. c) jumped
11. c) We played soccer at the park.
12. c) went
13. b) ate
14. b) did
15. b) chewed
16. c) will read
17. c) will go
18. c) will watch
19. c) will have finished
20. a) will finish
21. b) will finish
22. c) You should brush your teeth before bed.
23. b) should
24. c) should
25. c) They can swim in the pool.
26. a) can
27. c) will
28. c) We have played games at the party.

Pg. 107- Adjective Practice: Circle the noun in the sentence and then write the adjective that describes it in the box.

1.	She has a black cat.	black
2.	He is wearing a blue shirt.	blue
3.	The chicken is too spicy.	spicy
4.	The loud bell rang at 9 am.	loud
5.	I like chocolate cake.	chocolate
6.	We smelled the sweet flowers.	sweet
7.	They are sitting under a shady tree.	shady
8.	It's very hot today.	hot
9.	Look at the red balloon.	red
10.	I am smart.	smart

Pg. 108- Use adjectives to describe the pictures in complete sentences. ANSWERS MAY VARY

A small gray cat is in a grassy field with white and yellow flowers

A tiny black, brow, and white dog is being hugged.

The sky is orange, blue, and white. The bright sun is setting over the blue ocean.

The orange leaves are falling from the trees onto the winding path.

The girl has long hair and is wearing a yellow hat and a white shirt.

Pg. 109- Practice: Circle the person that is being described.

Brian is the short boy with the blue shirt.

Brian's brother Dennis is **taller** than Brian.

Brian's dad is the **tallest** in the family.

Pg. 111- Practice: Use the word provided to correctly complete the sentence.

1.	sweet	Cherries are sweeter than raspberries.
2.	cold	This is the coldest winter ever!
3.	short	I am shorter than my brother.
4.	tall	Mount Everest is the tallest mountain in the world.
5.	old	My grandfather is older than my grandmother.

Pg. 111- Adverb Practice: Read the paragraph. Draw a square around the verbs and circle the adverbs. Draw a line to connect the verb and the adverb that describes it.

Once upon a time, there lived a young girl named Sarah. She lived happily in a cozy cottage at the edge of the forest. Every morning, Sarah woke up early and eagerly to explore the woods. She wandered deep into the forest, marveling at the towering trees and chirping birds. Sarah walked carefully along the winding paths, listening intently to the rustling leaves. Suddenly, she spotted a colorful butterfly fluttering gracefully among the flowers. Excitedly, Sarah chased after the butterfly, laughing joyously as it danced away.

Pg. 112- Adverb & Adjective Practice: Use the word correctly to complete the sentence.

1. [lazy] The lazy cat stretched lazily on the windowsill.
2. [brisk] She walked briskly through the crowded market.
3. [beautiful] The beautiful flowers bloomed beautifully in the garden.
4. [confident] He spoke confidently during the presentation.
5. [happy] The happy bird chirped happily in the tree.
6. [melodious] She sang melodiously during the talent show.
7. [excited] The excited dog wagged its tail excitedly.
8. [energetic] They played energetically in the park all afternoon.
9. [graceful] The graceful butterfly fluttered gracefully in the breeze.
10. [quick] He ran quickly to catch the bus.
11. [loud] She sang loudly during the concert.
12. [happy] The children played happily in the park.
13. [careful] He drove carefully to avoid hitting the deer.
14. [fast] The train moved quickly through the countryside.
15. [quiet] They tiptoed quietly into the room.

Pg. 113- Adverbs of time Practice: Use the words from the box above to complete the story below.

Once upon a time, there was a little girl named Lily who lived in a small town. One chilly morning in November , Lily woke up excitedly because it was her birthday today. She couldn't wait to open her presents! Her parents told her she had to wait until later after breakfast. Lily ate her pancakes as fast as she could, and soon, she was tearing the wrapping paper off her gifts. She got a new bicycle, a dollhouse, and a big box of art supplies. Afterwards, she was outside riding her bike with her friends. Suddenly, Lily remembered she had to finish her homework before going to bed. But eventually , she forgot about her homework and fell asleep. Lily's mom woke her up, reminding her about her homework. Lily finished it immediately and crawled into bed, tired but happy after a wonderful birthday.

Pg. 114- Adverbs of place Practice

1. He searched [under | above] the bed for his lost toy.
2. The cat jumped [up | down] from the tree branch.
3. They sat [inside | outside] the cafe, enjoying their coffee.
4. The ball rolled [across | around] the playground.
5. She placed her backpack [near | far] the door before leaving.
6. The birds flew [high | low] in the sky.
7. The squirrel hid [behind | in front of] the tree trunk.
8. The children played [beside | under] the school building.
9. The fish swam [around | under] the coral reef.
10. They walked [along | across] the sandy beach, collecting seashells.

Pg. 116- Preposition Practice

1. Where is the cat? The cat is sitting (on) the rug.
2. Where is the basket? The basket is (next to) the desk.
3. Where is the pink blanket? The blanket is (under) the mom's feet..
4. Where is the clock? The clock is (between) the plant and the books.
5. Where is the lamp? The lamp is (over) the chair.
6. Where is the red chair? The chair is (in front of) the window.

Pg. 117- Sub Conjunctions Practice

1. because
2. if
3. while
4. before
5. while
6. until
7. although
8. because
9. when
10. before

Pg. 118- Adjective & Adverb Review Circle the noun and underline the adjective that describes it.

1. The red apple fell from the tree.
2. She has a beautiful smile.
3. It was a rainy day yesterday.
4. The small puppy followed me home.
5. He wears a blue shirt every Monday.

Pg. 118- Circle the verb and underline the adverb that describes it.

6. She speaks softly to avoid waking the baby.
7. He ran quickly to catch the bus.
8. The sun is shining brightly in the sky.
9. They played happily in the park all afternoon.
10. The dog barked loudly when the doorbell rang.

Pg. 118- Circle the best word to complete the sentence.

11. Sarah is the (fast | faster | fastest) runner on the team.
12. This is the (big | bigger | biggest) cake I've ever seen!
13. The elephant is (large | larger | largest) than the mouse.
14. Today is (hot | hotter | hottest) than yesterday.
15. The red car is (expensive | more expensive | most expensive) than the blue one.

Pg. 119- Circle the preposition in the sentence.

16. The book is on the table.
17. The cat jumped over the fence.
18. She walked to the store.
19. The keys are under the mat.
20. He sat beside his friend.

Pg. 119- Circle the best word to complete the sentence.

21. She arrived at the party (earlier | late) than expected.
22. The children played (outside | inside) until it started raining.
23. They went for a walk (yesterday | tomorrow) afternoon.
24. The store opens (soon | later) in the day.
25. The cat sleeps (under | above) the bed every night.
26. He finished his homework (quickly | slower) than usual.
27. We will have dinner (here | up) tonight.
28. She went to the library (yesterday | today) to borrow some books.
29. They waited (patiently | impatiently) for the bus to arrive.
30. The concert begins (soon | far) after sunset.

Pg. 120-124- Adjective Adverb Test

1. a) taller
2. b) tallest
3. a) loudly
4. b) quicker
5. c) most interesting
6. b) faster
7. a) on
8. a) to
9. a) later
10. c) beside
11. a) yesterday
12. c) best
13. b) bigger
14. b) under
15. a) across
16. b) quickly
17. c) among
18. c) most delicious
19. b) smarter
20. b) on
21. b) on
22. a) soon
23. b) down
24. c) happiest
25. b) higher

Pg. 125- List Comma Practice: Put the commas in the correct place.

1. I bought apples, oranges, bananas, and grapes at the grocery store.
2. She packed her clothes, shoes, socks, and toiletries for the trip.
3. We need to bring our pencils, notebooks, erasers, and textbooks to class.
4. He enjoys playing soccer, basketball, baseball, and tennis in his free time.
5. I visited Paris, London, Rome, and Madrid during my European vacation.
6. My favorite colors are red, blue, yellow, and green.
7. We need to buy bread, milk, eggs, and butter from the store.
8. The menu includes pasta, salad, pizza, and sandwiches for lunch.
9. She owns a cat, dog, rabbit, and hamster as pets.
10. They watched movies, played board games, sang songs, and danced at the party.

Pg. 126- Date Writing Practice: Write the date as Month Day, Year

What is today's date?	Answers vary
What was yesterday's date?	Answers vary
What is tomorrow's date?	Answers vary
When were you born?	Answers vary
When was your mom born?	Answers vary
When was your grandpa born?	Answers vary
When is Valentines Day?	February 14, 202?
When is White Day?	March 14, 202?
When is Pepero Day?	November 11, 202?
When is New Years Eve?	December 31, 202?

Pg. 127- Location Comma Practice: Put the comma in the correct place in the sentence.

1. Paris, France
2. Santa Monica, California
3. New York City, New York
4. Paris, France
5. London, England
6. Tokyo, Japan
7. Rome, Italy
8. Sydney, Australia
9.) Los Angeles, California
10. Beijing, China
11. Venice, Italy
12. Cairo, Egypt
13. Barcelona, Spain
14. Toronto, Canada
15. Arizona, USA

Pg. 126- Comma Review
This paragraph is missing 8 commas. Put them in the correct places.

Last summer I went on a memorable vacation with my family. We visited **France, England,** and Italy during our trip. On **July, 15 2023** we explored the Eiffel Tower in **Paris, France** and enjoyed breathtaking views of the city. Then, on **July 20, 2023**, we took a scenic boat tour along the River Thames in **London England**. Finally, on **July 25, 2023**, we marveled at the ancient ruins of the Colosseum in **Rome, Italy**. It was an unforgettable experience that I will always cherish.

Pg. 126-127- Circle the correct answer.

1. a) She enjoys reading, writing, and drawing in her free time.
2. a) The dog barked loudly, ran quickly, and jumped high.
3. a) They visited Paris, France, and London, England during their trip.
4. b) My favorite fruits are apples, oranges, and bananas.
5. c) He enjoys playing soccer, basketball, baseball, and tennis.
6. a) We need to buy bread, milk, eggs, and butter from the store.
7. a) She lives in New York City, New York.
8. b) They're going to visit Sydney, Australia, next month.
9. a) Have you been to Barcelona, Spain?
10. c) The Great Wall of China, Beijing is a must-see attraction.

Pg. 130- Read the sentence, if there is a mistake, circle it and write the correction on the line. If there are no mistakes, write "Correct".

1. She **want** to go to the store to buy some milk.	went
2. The cat sat on the mat, and licked its paws clean.	Correct
3. We're going **too** the beach for a picnic tomorrow.	to
4. They're going to Paris, London, and Rome.	Correct
5. He enjoys playing soccer, basketball, and tennis.	Correct
6. Have you been to **Barcelona Spain**?	Barcelona, Spain
7. The dog barked loudly, ran quickly, and jumped high.	Correct
8. She lives in New York City, New York.	Correct
9. My favorite fruits are **apples oranges**, and bananas.	apples,
10. The children played outside, until it started raining.	Correct

Pg.131-134- Punctuation Test

1. c) She enjoys playing soccer, basketball, baseball, and tennis.
2. b) My favorite colors are red, blue, yellow, and green.
3. a) He likes to read books, watch movies, and play video games.
4. b) The dog barked loudly, ran quickly, and jumped high.
5. b) They visited Paris, France, and London, England during their trip.
6. b) We need to buy bread, milk, eggs, and butter from the store.
7. b) She lives in New York City, New York.
8. a) The Great Wall of China, Beijing is a must-see attraction.
9. b) They're going to visit Sydney, Australia, next month.
10. a) Have you been to Barcelona, Spain?
11. a) The cat sat on the mat and licked its paws clean.
12. b) We visited Paris, France, London, England, and Rome, Italy.
13. b) I want to eat pizza, spaghetti, and salad for dinner.
14. a) They're going to the zoo tomorrow.
15. b) The party is on Friday, March 15th, 2025.
16. b) They plan to visit London, England, and Paris, France, during their vacation.
17. c) My birthday is June 12, 2008.
18. a) We'll be at the park at 2:00 p.m.
19. b) She lives in Chicago, Illinois.
20. a) Have you seen the movie Frozen 2?
21. c) We're going to the beach on Saturday, May 30th, 2024.
22. a) She wants to buy a new dress, shoes, and a hat for the party.
23. b) They traveled to Tokyo, Japan, and Seoul, South Korea, during their vacation.
24. a) My favorite subjects are Math, Science, and English.
25. b) We'll be arriving at the airport at 3:45 p.m. on Thursday, April 25th, 2024.
26. a) She wants to eat pizza, spaghetti, and salad for dinner.
27. c) His birthday is December 10, 2010.
28. a) They're planning to visit Washington D.C., and New York City during their trip.
29. a) The picnic will be at the park, near the lake.
30. c) The movie starts at 7:00 p.m. on Friday, May 3rd.

Pg. 135- Abbreviated Day and Month Practice: Complete the chart.

Sunday	→	Sun.	April	→	Apr
Monday	→	Mon.	May	→	X
Tuesday	→	Tue.	June	→	X
Wednesday	→	Wed.	July	→	X
Thursday	→	Thur.	August	→	Aug.
Friday	→	Fri.	September	→	Sept.
Saturday	→	Sat.	October	→	Oct.
January	→	Jan.	November	→	Nov.
February	→	Feb.	December	→	Dec.
March	→	Mar.		→	

Pg. 136- Abbreviated Title Practice: Rewrite the sentence with the correct abbreviation.

1.) Dr. Johnson

2.) Prof. Smith

3.) Capt. Thompson

4.) Rev. Davis

5.) Lt. Roberts

6.) Prin. Garcia

7.) Sgt. Brown

8.) Atty. Patel

9.) Col. Johnson

10.) Det. Ramirez

Pg. 137- Practice: Read the sentences. If there is a mistake, circle it and write the correction on the line. If there are no mistakes, write "correct".

1. Prof. Anderson teaches Biology. Correct
2. My uncle is a Lt. in the army. lieutenant
3. Mrs. Lopez is giving a presentation. Correct
4. Capt. Smith will be piloting the plane to New York. Correct
5. Dr. Brown is a renowned surgeon at the hospital. Correct

Pg. 137- Abbreviations for Units of Measurement Practice: Write the word for the abbreviation shown.

in.	inch	kg.	kilogram
m	meter	g.	gram
c.	cup	L	liter
g.	gram	oz	ounce
yd	yard	tbsp	tablespoon
mL	milliliter	lb.	pound
tsp	teaspoon		
qt.	quart		

Pg. 138- Abbreviated Address Practice: Rewrite the addresses with all the possible abbreviations.

BTS Jungkook	
Loans Post Office Box #1062	Loans P.O. Box #1062
Donghwa Building Room. 201	Donghwa Bldg. Room 201
4 Wangsan-ro, Dongdaemun gu,	
Seoul, South Korea	Seoul, KOR
Dwayne "The Rock" Johnson	
224 Palermo Avenue	224 Palermo Ave.
COral Gables, Florida 33134	Coral Gables, FL 33134
United States of America	USA
Bruce Wayne	
1007 Mountain Drive	1007 Mountain Dr.
Gotham City, New Jersey 08701	Gotham City, NJ 08701
United States of America	USA
Elena Neves	
4321 Los Dinos Circle	4321 Los Dinos Cir.
Las Palmas, Canary Islands	
Spain	SPA
Doctor Stephen Strange	Dr. Stephen Strange
177A Bleecker Street	177A Bleecker St.
New York City, New York 10012	(NYC), NY 10012
United States of America	USA
Thor Odenson	
79 Tesseract Square	79 Tesseract Sq.
Tonsberg, New Asgard 3110	
Norway	NOR

Pg. 140- Abbreviations Review
Directions: Write the correct abbreviation for each given term.

1. Doctor	Dr.	12. Yards	yd
2. Thursday	Thur	13. Miss	Ms.
3. Kilometers	km	14. March	Mar
4. Mrs.	Misses	15. Avenue	Ave
5. January	Jan.	16. Wednesday	Wed
6. Professor	Prof.	17. June	June
7. Inches	in	18. Road	Rd.
8. Monday	Mon	19. September	Sept
9. Boulevard	Blvd	20. Kilometers	km
10. February	Feb	21. December	Dec.
11. Street	St.		

Pg. 141-142- Abbreviation Test

1. a) Jan.
2. a) Dr.
3. b) Thurs.
4. a) in.
5. b) St.
6. a) Feb.
7. b) Prof.
8. a) Ave.
9. b) mi.
10. b) Mon.
11. b) Mar.
12. b) Ms.
13. a) Rd.
14. a) km.
15. b) Thu.
16. a) Jun.
17. b) Mrs.
18. a) yd.
19. b) Wed.
20. b) Dr.
21. a) Blvd.
22. b) Dec.
23. b) in.
24. a) Thurs.
25. a) Sep.

Pg. 148-150- Letter Writing Test

1. a) December 25, 2023
2. a) 123 Maple Street
   Anytown, USA
   Postal Code: 12345
3. a) At the top left corner
4. b) The recipient's name and title
5. b) "Dear Mr. Smith,"
6. c) The main message or purpose of the letter
7. c) "Sincerely yours,"
8. b) Plan what you want to say.
9. c) "Could you please send me..."
10. c) At the end
11. c) Keeping sentences short and simple
12. a) No error
13. c) Sincerely, yours truly
14. a) Thank you for your help.
15. b) "I will send you a letter soon."

16. (informal) Hey Friend!
17. Geography, Culture, Language, Fun Facts, your Daily Life
18. (formal) sincerely, thank you, with sincere appreciation
19. Your background and qualifications, your interest in the position
20. What should be improved, the current state of the area, how improvements could be carried out and how it will affect the area.

Pg. 152-153- Titles Practice

1. Correct
2. Incorrect (To Kill a Mockingbird)
3. Incorrect ("Harry Potter and the Philosopher's Stone")
4. Incorrect (The Great Gatsby)
5. Correct
6. Incorrect (The Lord of the Rings)
7. Correct
8. Incorrect ("Thriller" by Michael Jackson)
9. Correct
10. Incorrect ("The Hunger Games" by Suzanne Collins)
11. Correct
12. Correct
13. Incorrect ("Let It Go" from Frozen)
14. Incorrect ("The Beatles: Yellow Submarine")
15. Correct
16. Correct
17. Correct
18. Correct
19. Correct
20. Correct

Pg. 154- Quotations Practice: Put in the missing quotation marks.

Sarah and her little brother Jake ventured into the enchanted forest. In a magical clearing, a wise old owl perched on a branch. "Who goes there?" it hooted. Sarah and Jake replied, "It's us, Sarah and Jake!" The owl welcomed them and asked, "What brings you here?" Sarah explained, "We're searching for the lost treasure of the forest". The owl nodded and said, "I can show you the way, but the journey will be perilous. Are you brave enough?" Sarah and Jake nodded eagerly. With the wise owl as their guide, they set off on their daring quest.

Pg. 155- Book Review

1. The cat purr loudly while sleeping.	purrs
2. She run quickly to catch the bus.	ran
3. They're going to the zoo on May 15, 2023.	Correct
4. The red, juicy apple fell from the tree.	Correct
5. He draw a picture of his family.	drew/draws
6. We should of finished the project yesterday.	have finished
7. The weather is to cold for outdoor activities.	too
8. The teacher gave everyone a gold star.	Correct
9. The puppy wag it's tail happily.	its
10. They're favorite movie is "The Wizard of Oz".	their
11. My sister goed to the store to buy some groceries.	went
12. The big, brown dog barked loud in the park.	loudly
13. She is reading a interesting book about space.	an
14. The students' brought their lunches to school.	students
15. Me and my friend went swimming at the pool.	My friend and I
16. The boy run fast to catch the baseball.	Correct

Pg. 156- Unscramble the sentence.

17. The children happily ran in the playground.
18. The cat sat on the roof of the house.
19. The choir sang loudly in.
20. They played happily at the park.
21. Her homework did yesterday afternoon.
22. The family walked happily along the beach.
23. The dog wagged its tail happily.
24. The books were neatly arranged on the bookshelf.

Pg. 157- Circle the best answer

25. bigger
26. elephants
27. ran
28. books
29. interesting
30. sunny
31. oven
32. finished
33. peacefully
34. their
35. happy
36. went
37. brown
38. pretty
39. wagged
40. movie

Pg. 158-161- Book Test

1. c) Running in the park.
2. b) On the table.
3. b) The cat chased the mouse.
4. c) She walked to the store, she bought some milk.
5. c) She went to the store, and she bought some milk.
6. a) I like to play soccer, my favorite team is Real Madrid.
7. a) Eiffel Tower
8. a) goose
9. c) mouse
10. c) children
11. c) New York City
12. a) boxes
13. a) I
14. b) which
15. a) she
16. c) himself
17. a) me
18. c) himself
19. c) went
20. b) smell
21. a) go
22. b) jumped
23. c) happiest
24. c) fluently
25. b) bluer
26. b) quickly
27. b) I like to eat apples, oranges, and bananas.
28. b) The event will take place on July 4, 2022.
29. b) He bought milk, bread, and eggs.
30. b) The event will take place on October 31, 2024.
31. b) She lives in New York, New York.
32. a) Mon.
33. a) Jan.
34. a) Sun.
35. b) Dear Sir or Madam,
36. b) Sincerely,
37. b) Hi,
38. b) Best wishes,
39. a) The teacher said that "the test is tomorrow."
40. b) She said, "I am hungry."
41. a) She said, "I am hungry."
42. b) The teacher said that "the test is tomorrow."

REFERENCES

The Measures of Academic Progress (MAP) Test is a computerized assessment used to evaluate students in grades kindergarten through 12th in reading, language usage, math, and, for higher levels, science. Unlike standardized tests, the MAP Test assesses students based on their individual abilities rather than their grade level.

The MAP Test consists of sections covering reading, language usage, math, and science, with each section containing an average of 45 questions in various formats, including fill-in-the-blank, drag-and-drop, and multiple choice. What sets the MAP Test apart is its adaptive nature: the difficulty of the questions adjusts based on the student's responses. As the student progresses through the test, questions become progressively more challenging, but if an incorrect answer is provided, subsequent questions become easier. This adaptive approach ensures thorough evaluation of the student's knowledge, enabling administrators to accurately monitor progress, tailor instruction to individual needs, and pinpoint areas requiring additional support.
Writing Styles: There are several different writing styles commonly used in academic settings.

Persuasive or Argumentative: This writing style makes an argument for one particular opinion and gives evidence to support their idea. Topic examples: What is your opinion on women in the military? What is your favorite ice cream flavor? IS homework important?

Expository: This style of writing describes a topic in great detail without bias. Topics include: Should social media be censored? Define the meaning of friendship.

Descriptive: This style of writing should paint a picture in the mind of the reader. You are able to use more imagery in this style of writing and not so much focus is placed on facts. Examples: Describe the perfect day. What would your dream home look like?

Narrative: This style tells a story about a personal experience that you have had. Topic examples include: Tell about a time you tried something new. How do you motivate yourself?

Personal or Reflective: Very similar to narrative essays but with a slightly different intent. You are still sharing a personal story however, you are diving more into how the situation made you feel instead of just retelling the story of what happened. Examples: What is an achievement that you are proud of? Tell about a time you failed.

Comparative: In this style you take two or more different ideas and find their similarities and oppositions. Examples: Are dogs or cats better pets? Why you should visit Mallorca instead of Barcelona.   apart is its adaptive nature: the difficulty of the questions adjusts based on the student's responses. As the student progresses through the test, questions become progressively more challenging, but if an incorrect answer is provided, subsequent questions become easier. This adaptive approach ensures thorough evaluation of the student's knowledge, enabling administrators to accurately monitor progress, tailor instruction to individual needs, and pinpoint areas requiring additional support.

Writing Styles: There are several different writing styles commonly used in academic settings.

IS PREP
LANGUAGE USAGE (GRAMMAR)

1판 1쇄 발행 2024년 6월 25일

지은이 신종철

편집 이새희
마케팅 • 지원 김혜지

펴낸곳 (주)하움출판사 펴낸이 문현광

이메일 haum1000@naver.com 홈페이지 haum.kr
블로그 blog.naver.com/haum1000 인스타 @haum1007

ISBN 979-11-6440-624-1(13740)

좋은 책을 만들겠습니다.
하움출판사는 독자 여러분의 의견에 항상 귀 기울이고 있습니다.
파본은 구입처에서 교환해 드립니다.